Practical Ideas, Games and Activities for the Primary Classroom

Other titles in the series

Practical Ideas, Games and Activities for the Primary Classroom

Paul Barron

PEARSON
Longman

Harlow, England • London • New York • Boston • San Francisco • Toronto
Sydney • Tokyo • Singapore • Hong Kong • Seoul • Taipei • New Delhi
Cape Town • Madrid • Mexico City • Amsterdam • Munich • Paris • Milan

Pearson Education Limited
Edinburgh Gate
Harlow CM20 2JE
United Kingdom
Tel: +44 (0)1279 623623
Fax: +44 (0)1279 431059
Website: www.pearsoned.co.uk

First edition published in Great Britain in 2008

© Pearson Education Limited 2008

The right of Paul Barron to be identified as author of this work has
been asserted by him in accordance with the Copyright, Designs and Patents Act 1988.

ISBN: 978-1-4058-5945-5

British Library Cataloguing in Publication Data
A CIP catalogue record for this book can be obtained from the British Library

Library of Congress Cataloging in Publication Data

Barron, Paul.
    Practical ideas, games, and activities for the
primary classroom / Paul Barron.
        p. cm.
    ISBN 978–1–4058–5945–5
    1.   Education, Elementary – – Activity programs. I.
Title.
    LB1592.B37 2009
    372.13—dc22

2008026108

10 9 8 7 6 5 4 3
13 12 11 10

Set by 30
Printed and bound in Great Britain by Henry Ling Ltd, Dorchester, Dorset

The Publisher's policy is to use paper manufactured from sustainable forests.

Contents

Introduction

Purpose

This book provides a wealth of activities, ideas and games for use in the primary classroom. It is unique in its approach in that it offers such a wide range of exercises, on so many subjects, with a pure focus on practical, useable ideas. It will offer you inspiration whether you are a new or an experienced teacher by suggesting workable and adaptable ideas for use in many areas of the curriculum and in daily classroom life. This book is a quick and easy way to access fresh ideas to engage children, and provide you with new teaching tools and tactics to add to your collection.

Whether you are preparing to teach a lesson, play a game or create a display, *Practical ideas, games and activities for the primary classroom* is ready to offer you an exciting gem of an idea.

How to use this book

The ideas have been grouped into subject area chapters; however, you will find that many have great cross-curricular potential. There are chapters which deal with curriculum subjects and others which focus on extra-curricular areas such as 'Display'. This book is not intended to be a complete syllabus for the National Curriculum. It is designed to be dipped in and out of when you need inspiration, when you need a new and exciting way to deliver a learning objective or when you want to try something new to keep your children stimulated.

Practical ideas is designed with the busy teacher in mind: it is easy to navigate, the explanations are clear and brief, and the pages have an easy-to-follow layout.

Each chapter begins with an introduction, and is arranged with activities most suited to Key Stage 1 first (KS1), followed by those for all ages (KS1, KS2), and finally those best for Key Stage 2 (KS2). These classifications are only intended to be a general guide. The activities are versatile and adaptable across the age range, and many include variations which will help to differentiate the activity from its original version. Key Stage 2 teachers will find lots of useful ideas in the KS1 activities and vice versa.

Page layout

Headings indicate the subject of each activity and there is a brief description
under the title to give you an idea of what is to come. The 'Learning Objectives'
are linked to the National Curriculum programmes of study. 'Resources' that you
will need for each activity are listed (most of the things you will need can be
found in school or can be easily acquired elsewhere). 'What to Do' contains
clear and concise instructions on how to deliver the exercise as well as
photographs and diagrams. 'Variations' gives alternatives, cross-curricular angles
and ideas for extension and differentiation of the activity.

Acknowledgements

A big thank you to Katie, Jack and Daisy for their constant support and
encouragement. I should also like to thank the children of Larkfields Junior
School (Nottingham) and Luxulyan School (Cornwall) whose work has been
photographed for this book.

'To my Grandad, a great man, who showed so much faith in me throughout his life.'

Chapter 1
Art & DT

Art & DT

In this section you will find lots of design-based activities, some of which can be taught as stand-alone lessons and others which can be presented as longer-term projects.

With today's wide curriculum to deliver, many teachers regret that creative subjects such as Art and DT are neglected in favour of other topics. A way to remedy this is to exploit the numerous cross-curricular links that can be made with subjects such as English, Mathematics and Science.

Cross-curricular examples:

- Frame It (see page 32). This project has strong connections with Mathematics through the use of measuring skills (Ma3). In a using and applying Mathematics context you could allow the children to measure and calculate how much wood they will need for their frame and decide what lengths it will need to be cut to. They could then calculate the cost of their frame if given the price per metre of the wood. Follow this by assisting the children with measuring, marking out and sawing the required lengths to make the frames.

- Uniform (see page 27). This activity links well with Science through the area of materials and their properties (Sc3). In an investigative Science context the children could experiment with different materials to assess their suitability for use in a new school uniform. They could then use their findings as a basis for their design choices.

- Adverts (see page 7). This idea has many links with English via the areas of Speaking and Listening (En1) and Writing (En3). Many stages of the Adverts project could be completed as part of Literacy lessons. The initial stage of evaluating existing adverts provides many opportunities for speaking and listening, while also asking the children to think about the language used, its purpose and effectiveness. The children can then use their understanding and findings to develop their own adverts.

Magic Carpet

This is an exciting textiles project where children design and make a magic carpet. The pupils create one square each, which will be fixed together to make a beautiful collaborative piece of work.

Suitable for

KS1

Aims

- To design and make artefacts.
- To develop ideas by shaping materials and pulling together components.
- To develop control of tools and techniques.

Resources

- Pencils/crayons/felt-tips
- Fabric pens
- Fabric paints
- Fabrics/textiles/ribbons
- Material squares suitable for fabric paints or sewing
- Sewing tools

What to do

1. Tell or read a story which involves a magic carpet and wishes (e.g. Aladdin). Show the children pictures of magic carpets or real patchwork rugs/blankets, then discuss elements such as pattern, texture and colour.

2. Explain to the children: 'We are going to make a magic carpet! Everyone will need to make one part of the carpet. You will need to decorate your part of the carpet very beautifully if it is going to be magic! You can use fabric paints/pens and sew things on to your square.'

3. The children make their square with supervision and assistance if using needles to sew. Once the squares are complete they can either be joined together at the edges, or attached to a large piece of material by sewing, stapling or gluing the corners.

4. When the magic carpet is finished, it can be used in a PSHE game where the children make and share wishes as they sit on it.

Variations

- Ask the children to create their design and refine their ideas before making their carpet square.
- The children could make their own individual small magic carpets.

Adverts

Adverts is an activity where children look at the importance of design, colour and text in the world of advertising. The children will use their findings to create an effective advert for a product.

Suitable for

KS1, KS2

Aims

- To investigate and combine materials to match the purpose of the work.
- To develop control of tools and techniques.
- To combine text, graphics and colours effectively.

Resources

- Selection of adverts for discussion
- Adverts collected by the children from newspapers/magazines
- Art paper
- Access to computer and printer
- Flipchart/Whiteboard
- Coloured paper
- Felt-tips/coloured pencils/paint/ink pens

What to do

1. Display a selection of product adverts from newspapers or magazines. Ask the children to identify key features of the adverts. You could list these on a flipchart or whiteboard, i.e. use of colour, shape, photographs, graphics, text, headlines.

2. Allow the children to work in small groups to examine and evaluate adverts which they have collected at home. You could ask

the children to decide which advert is their favourite and why. Invite the children to share their favourite adverts with the other groups and explain their reasoning for their choices. You could write a list of points they make on their favourites to help understand what goes into a good, effective or successful advert.

3. Explain to the children: 'You are going to design a magazine advert for a product. You should take into account the list of ideas which we have made on what makes a good advert.'

4. The product to be advertised could be chosen by the children (from a list of items invented by the children) or chosen by the teacher.

5. The children begin the design process by deciding on colours, text, logos, etc. and creating an initial sketch which they can refine and develop into a final design. You could allow the children to choose the most appropriate tools and techniques for creating their final advert.

Variations

- The children could create an advert for a product which they have designed and made themselves as part of a DT, Art or Science project.
- The adverts could incorporate graphics or patterns designed using a computer art software package.
- The activity can be extended by allowing children to design and make television or radio adverts to accompany their project.

Album Artwork

Album Artwork is an exciting project where children design and make their own album cover insert for a music CD. The designs can incorporate elements of graphics, drawings, collage and photography.

Suitable for

KS1, KS2

Aims

- To design and make images.
- To explore the roles of artists and designers.
- To develop control of tools and techniques.

Resources

- Selection of existing album covers (or pictures of album covers)
- Template sheets showing CD insert dimensions
- Pencils/crayons/felt-tips
- Collage materials
- Empty CD cases (optional)
- Digital camera (optional)

What to do

1. Display a selection of existing album covers. This selection could be comprised of older/classic/iconic album covers (The Beatles – *Abbey Road*/*Sgt Pepper's*, Pink Floyd – The *Dark Side of the Moon*) and modern album covers (Gorillaz – *Demon Days*, Mika – *Life in Cartoon Motion*, Keane – *Under the Iron Sea*).

2. Invite the children to discuss their favourite album covers from the selection and feed back their thoughts to the rest of the class. You could list the children's ideas and make a note of the different techniques used to create effective covers, e.g. photography, colour, shape, symbolism, animation and lettering.

3. Explain to the children: 'You are going to be designing and making your own album cover for a CD. You will need to think of a name for your artist/performer (the children could use their own name or an existing artist), a title for the album and what the album cover is going to look like.'

4. In the first session, the children could sketch and refine their design ideas for their album cover. They should experiment with lettering and the arrangement of the images until they are happy with a final version. The children could complete their final design on a template which has the appropriate dimensions for a CD insert.

5. In the following session, the children make their album cover insert using techniques appropriate to their design. This could include textiles, paint, photography, computers, collage, etc.

6. Once the album covers are complete, the class can work in groups to evaluate their own and other children's album covers.

Variations

- You could insert the completed album covers into actual CD cases. You may need to take digital photographs of covers which contain paint, textiles or collage. These photographs can then be resized and printed before being inserted into the CD case.
- A different approach could be to select an existing album cover which the children have to redesign in their own style.
- Ask the children to bring in their own favourite album covers from home for analysis.

Here are some examples that my students produced. These and additional images are available to view/download from the companion website at **www.pearsoned.co.uk/barron**.

Coat of Arms

Coat of Arms is an interesting activity in which children will design and make their own family crest. It encourages them to think about themselves and their families, while creating a unique symbolic design.

Suitable for

KS1, KS2

Aims

- To use symbols and colour to reflect meaning.
- To understand the history and significance of heraldry.
- To develop control of tools and techniques.

Resources

- Pictures/photos of coats of arms
- A3 size art/watercolour paper
- Paints/coloured pencils/felt-tips/pastels/chalks
- Scissors
- Textiles/felt (optional)

What to do

1. Display a selection of Coat of Arms pictures/photographs. These can be found easily by using an internet search engine. The selection could include the school, county and family coats of arms.

2. Start a discussion to identify the key features of the pictures. Then begin to introduce the history of heraldry, i.e. where the colours,

shapes and symbols have personal significance in the design of the Coat of Arms.

3. Explain to the children: 'You are going to be designing and making your own Coat of Arms/family crest. You will need to choose a shape for the shield, symbols/animals for decoration and colours. You might want to include your initials in your design. Your Coat of Arms should reflect you and your family.'

4. You could allow the children to research heraldry symbols and shapes before beginning to design and make a Coat of Arms.

5. To make the Coat of Arms the children need to fold a piece of art paper in half lengthwise, draw the outline of one side of their chosen shield shape, cut it out and fold out the page. The design can be decorated using paints, coloured pencils, felt-tips, pastels or chalks.

Variations

- You could provide younger children with pre-drawn shield outlines to be cut out and decorated.
- The Coat of Arms can be made using textiles such as felt.
- Consider allowing the children to use the internet to find relevant images, symbols or pictures, print them and stick them on to their design.

These and additional images are available to view/download from the companion website at www.pearsoned.co.uk/barron.

Grid Painting

Grid Painting is a large-scale art project where children take small pieces of a painting or image, and make their own version. The children's pieces are recombined to make a stunning display.

Suitable for

KS1, KS2

Aims

- To design and make images.
- To explore and evaluate works of art.
- To develop control of tools and techniques.

Resources

- Copy/print of chosen painting (large)
- Printout of chosen painting marked out into grid sections
- Printout of chosen painting divided into grid sections and cut up into individual pieces (enough for 1 per child or partner group)
- Square-shaped pieces of art paper
- Pencils/crayons/felt-tips
- Collage materials
- Paint and brushes
- Computer and art software package (optional)
- Area suitable to display work

What to do

1. Display a large copy of the chosen painting, e.g. *Starry Night* by Van Gogh. This image could be a print of the painting or a digital image displayed on a whiteboard. Invite the children to evaluate the painting with a partner and discuss elements such as: colour, line, texture, shape, materials and subject. (These discussion topics should be differentiated according to the ability of the children.)

2. Allow the children to report back on their discussions and then share likes and dislikes about the painting, giving appropriate reasons.

3. Explain to the children: 'We are going to be creating a new, large version of the painting. The painting is going to be divided up into sections of equal size. You will make your own version of the square which you are given on a larger square of paper. You will need to enlarge the image to fill the whole of your square. You can choose the materials which you want to use to decorate your square. (Options: paint, pencil, chalk, pastel, computer art, textiles or collage.) Once all of the squares are complete, we are going to build them up in rows to create our own version of the painting.'

4. Remember to label the grid sections on the printout of the painting, and label the squares of art paper given to the children accordingly, e.g. (Row A/Square 1/This Way Up). This makes the reconstruction of the children's squares much easier.

5. Once the display has been built using the children's squares, it can be compared with the original painting.

Variations

- Try encouraging the class to use a variety of media/materials. This looks very effective when the artwork is displayed, i.e. some squares decorated with textiles, some with paint and others with collage.
- Younger children may find the activity easier if the piece of the painting which they are copying from is enlarged to match the size of their square. Older children should be able to cope with enlarging the image to scale by themselves.
- The activity could be carried out in smaller groups. Each group can have their own painting, which is divided up into sections, to recreate. The groups could be given a selection of paintings by the same artist.
- Why not allow some or all of the children to recreate their section of the painting using an art software package on a computer?

Illuminated Names

Illuminated Names is an interesting activity where children learn about the art of illumination and go on to create their own illuminated initials.

Suitable for

KS1, KS2

Aims

- To use imagination to explore ideas.
- To develop control of tools and techniques.
- To explore the roles of designers/artists.

Resources

- Pictures of illuminated letters or books containing illuminations
- Rulers/set squares/protractors
- Pencils/crayons/felt-tips/paint – including metallic colours (especially gold)
- Art paper
- Squared paper (optional)
- Access to computers for research (optional)

What to do

1. Introduce the project by displaying and discussing a range of illuminated letters (examples can be easily located on the internet). Explain to the children: 'An illumination is a decoration which enhances a written page. The word "illumination" means "to fill with light". An illuminated letter is the first letter of a page or paragraph. It is always enlarged and in colour. The images used to decorate the illuminated letters include animals, plants, symbols and mythological creatures. You are going to design and make an illuminated letter using one of your initials.'

2. You may wish to demonstrate: how to draw out a capital letter using a ruler, how to decorate using a theme such as animals and how to use colour to create patterns.

3. Once the children have drawn the outline of their letter, they should think about a theme, and begin to decorate their illumination. The themes chosen for the illuminations could be selected to reflect some personal details or interests which the children have. The class could be encouraged to create several design ideas and then choose to make their favourite into a full illumination.

Variations

- Why not provide photocopied templates of letters for the children to decorate/illuminate if they find it difficult to draw an effective letter shape by themselves?
- An illumination could be created to decorate a piece of the children's English work.
- You could allow the children to research the topic and find images using the internet before beginning the design process.

These and additional images are available to view/download from the companion website at **www.pearsoned.co.uk/barron**.

Money Maker

Money Maker is a great activity where children design and make their own banknotes. This provides many opportunities for cross-curricular links with Geography (countries), Numeracy (money problems) and PSHE (heroes).

Suitable for

KS1, KS2

Aims

* To develop understanding of pattern, shape and texture.
* To explore the role of artists.
* To develop control of tools and techniques.

Resources

* Selection of banknotes or pictures of banknotes
* Art paper in banknote sizes
* Coloured pencils/felt-tips
* Black ink pens
* Polystyrene printing sheets (optional)
* Printing inks, trays and rollers (optional)
* Access to internet and printer (optional)

What to do

1. Introduce the topic of money to the children by discussing what money is and how it has evolved. Allow them to examine a variety of banknotes or pictures of banknotes. You could highlight: the value of the notes, the people/items featured on the notes, patterns, paper quality, security features and colour coding.

2. Draw attention to the people/items featured on the back of the notes and explain their significance and achievements. You could ask the children to consider who they would include on the back of a new banknote, and why. The children could research their choice of person using the internet and print a photograph of them to be copied in a new note design.

3. Each class member designs their own new banknote, considering both sides of the note. The teacher could encourage the children to choose a significant person, e.g. a hero and their achievements, to feature on the reverse of the note, or they could use an image of themselves and one of their achievements. Once a final design has been completed, the children can make their notes using art paper, coloured pencils and ink pens to outline key features.

4. Finally, the children can share their note with the other children and explain their choice of the person featured on the reverse.

Variations

- The final designs could be printed using inks rather than drawn. The children would need to carefully mark out their design on to polystyrene printing sheets, remembering to mark any writing or numbers in reverse.
- The children could research a hero as part of PSHE, or for homework, before using that person's image in a note design.
- A range of coins could also be designed and made from clay or other modelling materials.

Nature Collage

Nature Collage is a fantastic opportunity for a class to collect materials from nature and create designs. The children will explore pattern, texture and arrangement to create an environmental work of art.

Suitable for

KS1, KS2

Aims

- To investigate and combine materials to match the purpose of the work.
- To compare methods and approaches in their own and other artists' work and say what they think and feel about them.

Resources

- Photographs of art by Andy Goldsworthy
- Collection of nature materials
- Digital camera
- Large sheets of paper

What to do

1. Display a range of photographs of artwork by Andy Goldsworthy, a British environmental artist. These can be found easily by using an internet search engine. The photographs should include works of art which are made with materials from nature.

2. Lead a discussion to identify the key features and themes of the photographs. Explain to the children: 'You are going to be creating our own nature collage. You will need to take time to carefully arrange the materials from nature into a shape or pattern which looks effective. Once you are happy with your design, you will take a photograph of it which will be printed out and displayed.'

3. The children could then go and collect materials for their nature collage such as: twigs, leaves, pine-cones and seed pods. The children will need to be given clear rules on what to gather and be supervised during this collection. If there is no possibility of finding nature materials on the school site, then a trip could be arranged to do this at a nearby park, the teacher could collect and bring in nature materials, or the children could bring in materials collected at home with parental supervision.

4. Once the materials have been collected, the children can arrange them outside on a range of surfaces (grass/soil/concrete) or alternatively they can arrange their collage on large sheets of paper inside the classroom. They should be encouraged to experiment with different arrangements before selecting their final design to be photographed.

5. The children must wash their hands after creating their collage.

Variations

- The children can create a nature collage individually, in pairs, in groups or as a whole class. Remember that the larger the collage becomes, the higher you will need to be to take a photograph!
- The teacher may wish to give younger pupils a smaller selection of materials to arrange, or make a pattern on paper by writing down the names of materials such as twigs/leaves/cones. The children then put the appropriate object down on the name to create their collage.

These and additional images are available to view/download from the companion website at **www.pearsoned.co.uk/barron**.

Self-portrait Ideas

Self-portraits are a traditional art activity. Children enjoy creating self-portraits and they provide a useful opportunity to assess artistic skills and progress.

Suitable for

KS1, KS2

Aims

- To record and represent ideas from firsthand observation.
- To explore self-image.
- To develop control of tools and techniques.

Resources

Dependent on which idea is used:
- Overhead projector and paper
- Paint and brushes
- Chalks/charcoal/pastels
- Digital camera and printer

What to do

Here are some suggestions for self-portrait activities:

Silhouettes Use an overhead projector to create individual silhouettes of the children's heads. Each child will need to stand in between the projector and a board with some paper attached to it. The child must stand side-on to give a profile image on the paper. The outline of the image is drawn around by you, or a child, on the paper. The child then cuts out their self-portrait silhouette. The cut-out silhouette can then be used in a number of ways:

- a collage can be built up on the head silhouette which reflects the child's personality
- paint or colour can be used to decorate the image in a realistic or surrealist fashion
- the image can be transferred on to black paper, then mounted on white paper to give a traditional silhouette effect.

Photographs Use a digital camera to take individual photographs of the children; these can be head-shots or full body photos. Why not ask the children to express a feeling or emotion with their faces and bodies? Once the photos have been printed, the children can use them to create a self-portrait in pencil, paint, pastel, etc. This option is an alternative to the traditional method of children using a mirror to view themselves.

Moving Photographs Use a digital camera to capture an image of the children moving in some way: this could be walking, running, playing a sport, etc. The printed photograph can be used as the basis for a picture or painting of the child which explores the posture of the body when moving.

Identity Portraits The children complete a pencil/painted self-portrait on paper by using a photograph or a mirror. They leave a large space in the background of the portrait. They fill in the background with a number of elements:

- drawings of favourite things
- photographs or pictures of important life events
- decorative words which describe the child's personality
- drawings of items to symbolise the child's culture or heritage.

A variation on this idea is to create a 3D effect by using an open box/shoe box as a base for the piece. Objects can be attached as well as drawn and the portrait sits in the bottom of the box.

Templates You may wish to provide a range of basic face templates for younger children to use when completing self-portraits. They should be encouraged to look carefully at the shape of their face and choose an appropriate template, i.e. round, square, oval or heart-shaped. The portrait can then be completed using pencil, paint or pastel.

Variations

- A self-portrait can be done at the beginning, middle and end of each year to assess children's artistic progress and self-perception.

Skylines

Skylines is a great art activity where children create a landscape using paint and collage. The skylines can be in the setting of daytime, night-time or sunsets/silhouettes.

Suitable for

KS1, KS2

Aims

- To design and make images.
- To develop a sense of scale and perspective.
- To develop control of tools and techniques.

Resources

- Pictures/photos of skylines from around the world
- A3 size art/watercolour paper
- Paints – watercolour or ready mixed
- Coloured sugar paper or card (black if creating silhouettes)
- Scissors
- Glue

What to do

1. Display a selection of skyline pictures/photographs. These can be found easily by using an internet search engine. The selection could include skylines from around the world which the children might recognise, skylines of cities at different times, i.e. dawn/dusk/night and skylines which contrast, i.e. city/countryside/beach.

2. Lead a discussion about aspects of the pictures with the children including: horizon, colour, light, shadow, buildings/structures,

perspective, scale and how skylines look different at different times of day and night.

3. Explain/demonstrate how to do a colour-wash with paint to create a sky effect which reaches down to the horizon. This is followed by painting or sticking on a block of colour to represent the land which reaches up to meet the horizon. The teacher explains: 'While the paint on the background is drying, you can begin to make the buildings, structures and objects from paper which will be stuck on to your painting to create the skyline.'

4. The children could be given a particular focus for their work, i.e. a skyline at sunset, a skyline at night or a famous city skyline.

Variations

- Computer art software can be used to allow children to create the buildings, structures or objects to be printed and stuck on to their skylines.
- If creating famous city skylines, then the children could use the internet to locate and print photos of famous buildings or structures to be cut out and stuck on, e.g. the Eiffel Tower or Big Ben.
- The children could examine skylines or landscapes which have been painted by famous artists as a stimulus for their work, e.g. Monet – *Houses of Parliament* series.

Uniform

Uniform is a project where children design and make a new school uniform. The design process will include developing graphics, logos and colour choices. The children's designs can then be manufactured.

Suitable for

KS1, KS2

Aims

- To design and make artefacts.
- To generate ideas for products after thinking about who will use them.
- To explore the roles of artists and designers.
- To develop control of tools and techniques.

Resources

- Examples of existing school uniforms – clothing or pictures
- Pencils/crayons/felt-tips
- Plain t-shirts, baseball caps
- Fabric pens
- Fabric paints
- Fabrics/textiles
- Sewing tools

What to do

1. Lead a discussion on the purpose of having a school uniform and make notes of the relevant points made. This can be extended by noting the children's ideas on what constitutes a good school uniform.

2. The children should examine the existing school uniform or examples of uniforms from other establishments. The children can talk about colour, practicality, design, fashion, logos, quality and cost.

3. Explain to the children: 'You are going to be designing a new school uniform, taking into account all of the things we have discussed. When we have designed our uniforms, we will then have the opportunity to make them.' The teacher can then break down the task into manageable stages such as:

   - Initial Ideas.
   - Logo Design.
   - Final Design.
   - Skills Development – sewing techniques/using fabric paints or pens.
   - Making
   - Evaluating.

4. The children could be encouraged to design a complete uniform, but you may wish to focus the making stage on one particular item such as a t-shirt or baseball cap.

Variations

- The children could make miniature versions of their designs rather than making full-sized uniforms.
- Why not use computer art software to help the class develop designs and logos?
- The children could design and make a uniform for a local organisation and then show their finished pieces to them, e.g. supermarket, shop or bank.

Amazing Buildings

Amazing Buildings is an exciting project which gives children an insight into the world of architectural design. The class can let their imagination and creativity rule when designing their own buildings.

Suitable for

KS2

Aims

- To use imagination to explore ideas.
- To collect visual and other information to help develop ideas.
- To explore the roles of designers/architects.
- To begin understanding the balance between aesthetics and practicality.

Resources

- Photographs of existing buildings/structures – some which show imagination and beauty in their design, and some which do not
- Sketchbooks or booklets to record ideas in
- Rulers/set squares/protractors/metre sticks
- Art paper
- Access to computers for research (optional)

What to do

1. Introduce the project by displaying and discussing a range of photographs of buildings. This range could include examples of imaginative and classical architecture, e.g.

- Crooked House – Sopot, Poland 2004
- Taj Mahal – Agra, India 1632
- Sagrada Familia – Barcelona, Spain 1882 to present
- Petronas Towers – Kuala Lumpur, Malaysia 1998
- Space Needle – Seattle, USA 1961.

2. Explain to the children that they are going to be designing their own amazing building, but the first stage is to research an existing building. The children could use the internet to find pictures, details and facts about their favourite amazing building. You may wish to let them choose a building to research from a given list, or allow them to choose their own building. This research can be compiled in sketchbooks and accompanied by sketches of parts of the children's favourite buildings.

3. Once the research is complete, the children can begin to design their own building. They could work to a set design brief such as a theme, function or location for their structure. The design process should involve a cycle of creating, evaluating and refining ideas until a final design for the exterior is produced. More able children may wish to consider drawing their building design from different angles.

4. The final designs for the children's buildings can be drawn to scale on large pieces of paper. The children could add labels and notes to their research drawings which explain materials chosen and design choices/themes.

Variations

- The class could visit local buildings of architectural significance to explore design and use of materials.
- Why not allow the children to create a model of their amazing building?
- A visit to school by an architect could be arranged. The children could prepare questions to ask or have the chance to show their amazing building designs.

These and additional images are available to view/download from the companion
website at **www.pearsoned.co.uk/barron**.

Frame It

Frame It is an interesting project in which children study the effects which the construction and decoration of a frame can have upon a painting or photograph. Frames can be made for an existing artist's painting, or as a follow-on activity for a piece of the children's artwork.

Suitable for

KS2

Aims

- To investigate and combine materials to match the purpose of the work.
- To measure, mark out, cut, join and assemble materials.
- To develop control of tools and techniques.
- To learn how materials can be combined and mixed to create more useful properties, i.e. strengthening and joining.

Resources

- Postcard-sized prints of a painting (optional)
- Pieces/photographs of the children's artwork (optional)
- Selection of framed pictures/paintings/photos or pictures of elaborate frames from art galleries
- Lengths of wood or strong card suitable for cutting, joining and decorating
- Tools for cutting and shaping
- Painting equipment
- Staple gun
- Glue

What to do

1. Introduce the Frame It project by examining a range of frames with the children; these could be actual framed paintings/photographs or pictures of frames. Pictures of elaborate/antique frames can be found

on the internet. The children discuss the purpose of frames and how a frame can be used to add to the overall effect of a work of art.

2. Lead a focused task in which the children examine and experiment with different methods of joining wood or strong card, e.g. nailing, mitre joints, dowel joints, gluing, stapling, etc. The joining methods should be tailored according to the ability of the pupils. You should encourage them to explore methods they could use to make a freestanding frame stand up.

3. Explain to the children: 'You are going to make a frame for a piece of art. You will need to design the frame carefully, thinking about materials, decoration, joining and dimensions. Your frame needs to complement the piece of art which it is going to hold.'

4. Once the children have designed their frame, they can make it under supervision using appropriate tools and techniques. The piece of art/postcard print can be mounted into the frame and the finished pieces can be displayed in the form of a gallery and evaluated.

Variations

- You could measure and pre-cut lengths of wood or card for the children to build, join and decorate.
- The children could experiment by creating different frames using computer art software before choosing the one they want to make.

- The starting point for the project can be enhanced by visiting a local art gallery or museum to examine frames. A particular painting could then be chosen as the focus for the project.
- Why not combine this activity with Nature Collage, see page 20, by creating frames for photographs of the children's nature art.

These and additional images are available to view/download from the companion website at **www.pearsoned.co.uk/barron**.

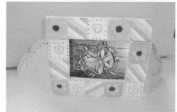

Real Life Paintings

Real Life Paintings is a super activity where children recreate a painting using a backdrop, props and themselves in costume. The resulting scene is photographed and compared with the original.

Suitable for

KS2

Aims

- To investigate and combine materials to match the purpose of the work.
- To explore the roles and aims of artists.
- To develop control of tools and techniques.

Resources

- Painting/portrait chosen and displayed as the activity focus
- Large pieces of cardboard or paper for backdrop
- Fabrics/textiles for costume making
- Sewing tools
- Card/recycled materials for prop making
- Painting equipment
- Digital camera
- Face paints (optional)

What to do

1. Introduce the chosen painting to the children. By selecting a portrait with more than one subject/character you can ensure the involvement of many pupils in the final stages of the project, e.g. Seurat – Sunday afternoon on the Island of Grand Jatte; Monet – Poppy field in Argenteuil. Ask the class to discuss the painting and share their ideas on its themes and subject.

2. You could go on to explain some of the details and facts which are known about the painting and the artist. Such information can be found readily on the internet.

3. Once the children understand the subject and artist, you should explain: 'We are going to create a real life version of the painting. You will do this in groups by painting/making a backdrop which looks like the background of the painting, making costumes which you will wear to represent the characters/subjects of the painting and by making props to represent the items from the painting. Once you have built your real life painting, a photograph will be taken so that your version can be compared with the original.'

4. Allow the children to create their real life painting and ensure that they allocate jobs within their groups. They may need assistance or demonstrations on how to create costumes using material.

5. You may wish to allow the children to take turns at being the character/subject in the painting when the final photographs are taken.

Variations

- The children could carry out their own research into the painting and the artist using the internet or books, before the teacher shares what they have found out.
- The Real Life Painting photograph could also include a child who represents the artist painting the subjects.
- Why not invite groups to create different real life paintings, i.e. different paintings by the same artist, different paintings from the same period or paintings of similar subjects/scenes by different artists?
- Face paints could be used to help create the characters in the painting.

These and additional images are available to view/download from the companion website at **www.pearsoned.co.uk/barron**.

Chapter 2
English

Character
Creative Writing
Drama
Guided Reading
Story

English

In this section you will find some great ideas which aim to develop children's speaking and listening, reading and writing. Many are suitable for use in a cross-curricular way, and there are lots of practical and exciting concepts to help engage pupils in English/Literacy lessons.

The activities are arranged in five categories

1. Character
2. Creative Writing
3. Drama
4. Guided Reading
5. Story

Character Pie

Character Pie is a versatile activity that helps children to build characters for their writing which are complex and believable. It can also be used to analyse existing story characters.

Suitable for

KS1, KS2

Aims

* To develop and refine character ideas using planning.
* To imagine and explore characters' feelings and emotions.

Resources

* Character Pie to be drawn or displayed on whiteboard
* Individual Character Pie sheets (these could also be drawn in children's books or on whiteboards)

What to do

1. Explain to the children: 'You are going to be creating a character for a story. (You may wish to give them a specific genre for the story, i.e. an adventure story or a fairy-tale.) To help bring the character to life, you are going to be making a Character Pie. The Pie has four pieces: Loves/Hates/Worries/Dreams. You need to write ideas in each piece of the pie.'

2. You may wish to complete a shared Character Pie with the class to model the kind of responses needed. Here is an example for an adventure story:

The character:
- Loves: jungles, excitement and animals.
- Hates: spiders, lying and boredom.
- Worries: safety, money and has enemies.
- Dreams: finding treasure and being famous.

3. The children can complete their pie pieces in pairs or individually, and then begin to think about a name for their character.

Variations

- The Character Pie can be built on by using other character creation activities which examine character appearance and attributes (see Character Rating and Heads or Tails).
- The children could create a second character that is very different from the first.
- After developing characters, the class can then use them in extended writing.
- The Character Pie can be used to examine an existing character from a story which the children have studied.
- You can reduce or increase the number of sections in the pie depending on the children's ability.

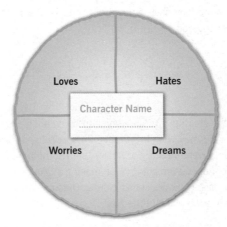

A template for this image is available to download from the companion website at **www.pearsoned.co.uk/barron**.

Character Rating

Character Rating is a useful activity which helps children to create detailed and more complex characters for their writing. It can also be used to analyse existing story characters.

Suitable for

KS1, KS2

Aims

* To develop and refine character ideas using planning.
* To imagine and explore characters' feelings and emotions.

Resources

* Character Rating chart to be displayed on whiteboard
* Individual Character Rating sheets (could also be drawn in children's books or on whiteboards)

What to do

1. Explain to the children: 'You are going to be creating a character for a story. (You may wish to give them a specific genre for the story, i.e. an adventure story or a fairy-tale.) To help bring the character to life, you are going to be rating your character. The rating chart has a list of character elements/attributes, and next to each one is a number rating area. The numbers go from 1 to 5, with 5 being the maximum or most. For example: if I circled the number 5 next to the word "Strong," this would mean that the character was very strong. If I circled the number 1 next to the word "Popular", this would mean that the character was very unpopular. If I circled the number 3 next to the word "Wealthy", this would mean that the character was neither very rich nor very poor.'

> **2.** The children can complete their Character Rating sheets in pairs or individually, and then begin to think about a name for their character.

Variations

- Character Rating can be built upon by using other character creation activities which examine character appearance and emotions/thoughts.
- Character Rating can be carried out at strategic points when a story is being read by, or to, the children. This will demonstrate that characters often change as a story develops.
- The children could create a second character that is very different from the first.
- After developing characters, the class can then use them in extended writing.
- You can reduce or increase the number of characteristics which the children have to rate, according to the type of character being created or depending on the children's ability.

Character Rating Grid Example

Character Name	Character Rating				
	Not very				Very
Tall	1	2	3	4	5
Strong	1	2	3	4	5
Wealthy	1	2	3	4	5
Intelligent	1	2	3	4	5
Powerful	1	2	3	4	5
Popular	1	2	3	4	5
Evil	1	2	3	4	5
Selfish	1	2	3	4	5
Attractive	1	2	3	4	5
Happy	1	2	3	4	5

These and additional images are available to view/download from the companion website at **www.pearsoned.co.uk/barron**.

Heads or Tails

Heads or Tails is a fun activity which helps children to build characters for their writing. By tossing a coin, the children decide on important details for their character. This is very useful for those who lack imagination in their writing or only include themselves or friends in their stories.

Suitable for

KS1, KS2

Aims

* To develop and refine character ideas using planning.
* To encourage children to create a variety of characters.

Resources

* Heads or Tails chart to be displayed on whiteboard
* Individual Heads or Tails sheets (could also be drawn in children's books or on whiteboards)
* Coins

What to do

1. Explain to the children: 'You are going to be creating a character for a story. (You may wish to give the children a specific genre for the story, i.e. an adventure story or a fairy-tale.) To help create character, you are going to be playing a game called Heads or Tails. The Heads or Tails chart has a list of character elements/attributes, and next to each one are two options. One option is under Heads, and the other is under Tails. You need to toss a coin for each element and circle the appropriate answer. For example: if I was deciding on the age of my character, tossed the coin, and it landed on heads, then my character would be a child. If the coin had landed on tails, then my character would have been an adult.'

2. The children can complete their Heads or Tails sheets in pairs or individually, and then compare their results with a partner.

3. Once the persona has been decided using the Heads or Tails sheet, then the children can use this information to create a detailed/accurate picture of their character.

Variations

- Heads or Tails can be built on by using other character creation activities which examine character appearance and emotions/thoughts (see Character Rating).
- The children could create a second character for use in their stories.
- After developing characters, the children can then use them in extended writing.
- Try differentiating the activity by leaving the Heads or Tails options boxes blank or with gaps, which the children must complete with appropriate options before tossing their coins.
- The character elements can be altered in accordance with the type of character being created, e.g. for a monster story the elements could be: Tail (Long or Short)/Teeth (Sharp or Round)/Skin (Scaly or Furry)/Claws (Long or Short)/Eyes (Fiery or Black), etc.
- Why not encourage the children to make and store a bank of character profiles which they can use whenever they are writing a story?

Heads or Tails Grid Example

	Heads	Tails
Age	Adult	Child
Sex	Boy	Girl
Hair Length	Long	Short
Hair Colour	Brown	_____ (write your own option here)
Eyes	_____ (write your own option here)	Blue
Country	England	_____ (write your own option here)
Attitude	Hardworking	Lazy

These and additional images are available to view/download from the companion website at **www.pearsoned.co.uk/barron**.

Useful character adjectives

adventurous	moody
aggressive	neat
beautiful	plain
bold	plump
boring	practical
calm	pretty
caring	rich
clever	rough
cunning	scruffy
cute	short
dainty	shy
funny	silly
good-looking	smart
grumpy	spotty
handsome	stupid
happy	sweet
hardworking	tall
helpful	ugly
honest	wrinkled
merry	

These and additional images are available to view/download from the companion website at **www.pearsoned.co.uk/barron**.

CV Building

CV Building is an effective activity which helps children to create detailed and complex characters by compiling a curriculum vitae (CV). This technique can also be used to analyse existing story characters.

Aims

- To develop and refine character ideas using planning.
- To create complex and believable characters.
- To imagine and explore characters' feelings and emotions.

Resources

- Example CV to be displayed on whiteboard
- Individual CV template sheets
- Computer and word-processing software (optional)

What to do

1. Explain to the children: 'You are going to be creating a detailed character for a story. (You may wish to give them a specific genre for the story, i.e. an adventure story or a fairy-tale.) To help bring the character to life, you are going to be compiling a CV (curriculum vitae) for them.'

2. You should outline what a CV is, its purpose and the common headings CVs contain.

3. Why not create a shared CV based on a familiar character as a model for the children? They can give suggestions for responses to the CV headings: full name, address, date of birth, education, qualifications, employment, hobbies and interests, etc.

4. The children then write their own CV for a new character in pairs or individually. Once completed in draft, the CVs could be edited and word-processed.

Variations

- CV Building can be used in conjunction with other character creation activities which examine character appearance and emotions/thoughts (see Character Pie and Character Rating).
- The children could create a second character's CV that is very different from the first.
- After developing characters, the class can use them in extended writing.
- CV Building can be used to examine an existing character from a story which the children are studying.

Blank CV template

Curriculum Vitae

Name: *D.O.B:*

Address:

Email Address:
Telephone Number:

Education:

Qualifications:

Employment:

Hobbies and Interests:

These and additional images are available to view/download from the companion website at **www.pearsoned.co.uk/barron**.

Strange Surroundings

Strange Surroundings is a fascinating activity which requires children to understand characters and stories very well. By placing a known character in the strange surroundings of a different story, the children will be able to explore a whole range of interesting outcomes.

Suitable for

KS2

Aims

- To show imagination through the language used to create emphasis, humour, atmosphere or suspense.
- To imagine and explore characters' feelings and emotions.
- To write effectively about characters entering new contexts.

Resources

- Individual whiteboards and pens
- List/pictures of suitable familiar characters (optional)
- List/pictures from suitable familiar stories (optional)

What to do

1. The children sit with a partner and draw a line which divides their whiteboard into two columns. Ask the pairs to write a list of characters which they know in one column. These characters can be from books, computer games, comics, films or TV. The second column is for the children to write a list of their favourite stories.

2. Invite the children to share some of their characters and stories with the class. These ideas can be recorded on the main whiteboard for the children to see.

3. Explain to the children: 'I wonder what would happen if we took one of the characters (e.g. Bart Simpson) and placed them in the strange surroundings of a new story (e.g. *Little Red Riding Hood*)?' Ask for ideas on how to change/adapt the story to accommodate its new character, and ideas on how to change/adapt the character to fit into the new story. An outline story plan can be made which includes details of how events change because of the new character.

4. The children work in pairs to choose a character and some strange story surroundings. They can then create a shared outline plan for their new story, which can be written up individually.

Variations

- The children could include a character which they have created themselves in Strange Surroundings, instead of using a known character.
- Why not allow the children to word-process their Strange Surroundings stories and convert them into a class book of the same name? Illustrations for the book could be completed in an art lesson.

Creative Writing Themes

Creative/extended writing is an essential activity where children are able to demonstrate their writing skills, i.e. composition, planning, punctuation, spelling, handwriting and presentation. The length of the extended writing session will depend on the age and ability of the children. Creative writing can be based on a topic/genre being studied or it can be a stand-alone lesson.

Suitable for

KS1, KS2

Theme Ideas

The Beach	Journey Into Space	The Haunted House
My Favourite Place	Imaginary Creatures	The Day I Won the Lottery
Bank Robbery Foiled	First Day at Wizard School	I Woke Up as a Superhero
Lost!	A Day at the Park	The Best Gift Ever
Animal Rescue	The Cowboy Saved the Day	A Trip to the Future
Jungle Adventure	Storm at Sea	Help!
Alien Encounter	The Secret Door	Three Wishes

Variations

- You may wish to write an opening sentence or paragraph on the chosen theme to help the children get started on their piece of writing. This shared opening could be written using the children's ideas.

- You may simply wish to give the theme for the piece of writing and let the children decide upon their own title for their work.
- A visual stimulus for writing such as a picture or photograph could be given to the children.
- You could provide a structured writing frame where the story is divided into sections, and each section has an opening sentence already written for the children to build on. Alternatively, provide a pictorial storyboard which sets out a clear beginning, middle and ending. The children would then need to write in responses to these pictures.
- It is good practice to suggest that the children spend the first minutes of their time creating a plan for their writing.
- The level of assistance given to the children will vary, i.e. completely unaided, use of dictionaries/word books allowed, help with spellings given, help with story development given.

Freeze-Frame

Freeze-Frame is a useful technique which can be used in conjunction with Guided Mime (page 54). By Freeze-Framing the action, the teacher and children are able to carefully examine posture and expression. Freeze-Frame gives an excellent opportunity for reflection on what is happening in the mime.

Suitable for

KS1, KS2

Aims

- To work in role to explore ideas, issues and texts.
- To use character and action to convey story, themes and emotions.
- To offer reasons and evidence for actions.

Resources

- Text for the narrator (any text appropriate for the age of the children)
- Space for children to move around safely
- Remote control – for use as a prop (optional)
- Digital camera (optional)

What to do

1. Explain to the children: 'You are going to be acting out a story. You are not allowed to talk or make any sounds while you act. Try to become a character by moving like them, using facial expression and acting out the events. I am going to be holding a remote control. When I press the Freeze-Frame button and say "Freeze-Frame," you need to freeze/pause in the exact position you are in at that moment. You need to freeze your bodies and your facial expression, and then think about how your character is feeling at that precise moment.'

2. Start reading the text (or telling the story) and allow it to continue until an appropriate point arrives for a Freeze-Frame. Once the children are frozen, you have the opportunity to comment on any children with good position or expression. You could also question the children about their character and reflect on the atmosphere created by the text.

3. Once the Freeze-Frame has been examined, you can press play on the remote control and the guided mime resumes until the next Freeze-Frame opportunity.

Variations

- The children could wear an item of costume or hold props to signify that they are in the role of a character.
- A digital camera can be used to take photographs of the children in their Freeze-Frame postures. The photographs can be used as a stimulus for writing, to show evidence of drama work or as part of a display about the text.
- Why not use the class reading book as the text or any appropriate story/genre being studied in Literacy lessons?

Guided Mime

Guided Mime is a great way of bringing text to life through drama. The teacher takes the role of narrator while the children act without speech. This technique is effective with a wide range of material, from nursery rhymes to complex novels.

Suitable for

KS1, KS2

Aims

- To work in role to explore ideas and texts.
- To use character and action to convey story, themes and emotions.

Resources

- Text for the narrator
- Space for children to move around safely
- Video camera (optional)

What to do

1. Choose an appropriate text for Guided Mime. It should contain plenty of actions and opportunities for the children to express their ideas through movement. You could improvise a story as the children act, or retell a story from memory, rather than read from a text. By choosing not to read from a text, you will be able to observe more of the children's acting work.

2. Explain to the children: 'I am going to read a story. You need to act out the story with your bodies. You are not allowed to talk or make

any sounds while you act. Try to become a character by moving like them, using facial expression and acting out the events.'

3. Read the text and keep note of any good techniques used by the children which can be praised and demonstrated at the end of the session. While reading, use your discretion in finding points at which to pause and allow the children to perform an action, or to allow tension to build.

Variations

- The children can wear an item of costume or hold a prop to signify that they are in the role of a character.
- The children could work in pairs if the text contains two obvious roles.
- Why not use a video recorder to capture the Guided Mime? This can be played back to the children to assist them in evaluating their performance.

Hot-Seat

Hot-Seat is an enjoyable and versatile activity which encourages children to act in role, and to ask and answer searching questions. It can be used to explore characters from many areas including books, films and poetry.

Suitable for

KS1, KS2

Aims

- To work in role to explore ideas and texts.
- To imagine and explore characters' feelings and emotions.
- To sustain conversation giving reasons for views or choices.

Resources

- Items of costume or props to signify character (optional)
- Individual whiteboards and pens (optional)

What to do

1. The children sit on chairs arranged in semicircle-shaped rows which face one chair at the front; this chair is known as the 'Hot-Seat'.

2. The child who sits on the Hot-Seat needs to stay in character. The remaining children take turns to ask the child in the Hot-Seat a question about something to do with their character.

3. Topics for questions can include the character's motivation, feelings, and reactions to or version of events. The child in the Hot-Seat should try and use their knowledge of the character and events to give insightful answers, but they should be encouraged to use a degree of improvisation and develop the character if possible.

4. The children take turns in the Hot-Seat to portray the same or different characters. You may need to demonstrate how to act in the Hot-Seat first before the children begin.

Variations

- The children can wear an item of costume or hold a prop to signify that they are in the role of the character.
- The children could make notes of questions to ask on whiteboards before the Hot-Seat session begins.
- You could provide the children with a list of questions to ask until they are familiar with the activity.

Snapshot

Snapshot is a versatile activity in which children work in groups. A Snapshot is made when children have worked together to create a still image which represents key moments, emotions or relationships from a text or other stimulus.

Suitable for

KS1, KS2

Aims

- To use dramatic techniques to explore ideas, issues and texts.
- To convey story, themes and emotions through posture and expression.
- To work cooperatively in a group situation.

Resources

- Text/stimulus for the Snapshots
- Space for children to create group freezes
- Digital camera (optional)

What to do

1. Explain to the children: 'You are going to be working in groups to create Snapshots. A Snapshot is a still picture which your group makes by placing your bodies in a certain way and using facial expression to show what is happening. A Snapshot can show feelings, key moments or relationships. Some people in your group might become the scenery or objects, while others become people. You need to be able to hold/freeze your Snapshot for at least one minute, and it needs to be silent.'

2. You may wish to build a Snapshot as a demonstration before the children go on to work in their groups. A discussion should take place about the importance of cooperating well with other group members to ensure success.

3. Explain the topic for the Snapshot freezes. This topic could be a key moment from a text which is being studied, relationships between characters in a text, a prediction of things to come in a text or the thoughts/dreams of a character.

4. Allow the children a period of time to discuss and practise their ideas for the Snapshot, and then say the word 'Snapshot'. At this point the children get into their positions and freeze.

5. Examine each group in turn and give constructive comments.

Variations

- The children can create items of costume or props to embellish their Snapshot.
- Why not try giving each group a different focus for their snapshot? The other groups could then try to work out what the Snapshot represents.
- A digital camera can be used to take photographs of the children in their Snapshot positions. The photographs can be used as a stimulus for writing, to show evidence of drama work or as part of a display about the stimulus.

Soundscape

Soundscape is an enjoyable activity where children work together as a class to create a landscape of sound. Soundscape is a great warm-up game for drama lessons.

Suitable for

KS1, KS2

Aims

- To use the voice creatively for different purposes.
- To work cooperatively in a group situation.

Resources

- Picture or film stimulus depicting appropriate scenes (optional)
- Tape recorder (optional)

What to do

1. Have the children sit in a circle and explain: 'We are going to be working together as a class to make a Soundscape. It is similar to painting a picture of a scene, but we are going to make the sounds of the scene instead. We are going to do this using our voices and body sounds.'

2. Introduce the topic for the Soundscape (a visual stimulus such as a photograph, painting or film clip with the sound muted can be used here). Some suggestions for Soundscape topics are: Stormy Seas/Supermarket/Airport/Beach/Car Journey/Industrial Factory/Rainforest/Sports Day.

3. Ask the children for suggestions of sounds which might be heard in the chosen scene/topic, and for ideas on how those sounds could be recreated using voices or body sounds. At this point you can choose to allocate certain sounds to groups of children within the circle, who are then asked to demonstrate their sound.

4. Once the children understand their role in the Soundscape, you can lead its creation by pointing to the groups in turn and building up the layers of sound. You can also use hand gestures to instruct the individual groups to be quieter or louder. One by one the teacher can make a 'stop' gesture to the groups which indicates that they should be silent; this continues until all of the groups have stopped.

Variations

- Try using a tape recorder to record the performance of the Soundscape, and then play it back to the children to evaluate its effectiveness.
- Why not choose an able child to lead the building of a Soundscape?
- You could set different stages within a Soundscape journey, e.g. for an Airport: Check-in/Boarding/Take off/Flight/Landing.

Guided Reading Activities

Guided Reading sessions can be made more engaging and exciting by using the activities and ideas listed here. The activities will be appropriate for most texts, although some of the ideas will not be suitable for non-fiction.

Suitable for

KS1, KS2

Activities|Ideas

Blurb. Write a new blurb/description for the text to feature on the back cover.

Author Letter. Write a letter to the author asking appropriate questions.

Book Votes. Each group member has two minutes to give a presentation on their favourite book. All children in the group vote on which book they would most like to read.

Desert Island Books. The children write a list of three books which they would take if they were going to be marooned on a desert island. They then give reasons for their choice to the rest of the group.

Book Quiz. Host a quiz on story characters, facts or plot.

Comparing Texts. Examine two guided reading books or texts. Which do the children like the best? What are the similarities and differences?

Synonyms. The children choose a descriptive word from the text, write it down and, using a thesaurus, write down five synonyms and antonyms for that word. Repeat without using a thesaurus.

Character Study. Write a description of a character: their looks, the way they dress, the way they talk and their personality. Draw a picture of the character.

Imagery. Choose a descriptive passage from which the children make a list of examples of vivid imagery – similes, metaphors, alliteration, noun phrases etc.

Atmosphere. The children list the words and phrases used to create an atmosphere in the text.

Feelings. The children write about what a character might be thinking or feeling at any stage of the story. This could be written in the first person, or in a speech bubble.

Predictions. What might happen next? This can be done at any stage of the story. The children could write in the form of a story plan in boxes.

Reactions. How did the book make you feel? Explain.

Recommendations. Who else should read this book? Why? Who shouldn't read this book? Why?

Quotations. The children assemble a collection of key quotations from the text and explain their choices.

Guided Reading Questions

In Guided Reading sessions, the following list of questions can be used to assess understanding and promote discussion. The questions are aimed mainly at fiction texts, and they should be differentiated according to the ability of the children in the guided reading group.

Suitable for

KS1, KS2

Questions about books

- How did you feel about the book when you finished it?
- Did the story keep your interest from the start?
- Was the ending a surprise?
- Could the story have ended differently?
- Which character was your favourite and why?
- Have you read any similar books?
- Would you recommend the book to someone else?
- Why did the author choose the title?
- What type of story is this? How do you know?
- Was there anything that you disliked about the book?
- Was there anything in the book which puzzled you?
- Has anything that happens in the book ever happened to you?
- Where did the story happen?
- Who was narrating the story? How do we know?

Questions about the children as readers

- How do you choose a book?
- Do you always finish every book which you read?
- Do you read more than one book at a time?
- Have you ever read the end of the book before you got there?
- Which book character would you most like to meet?
- Do you re-read books?
- Who is your favourite author?
- What type of story do you like to read?

Story Sequencing

Story Sequencing includes a range of basic activities which are aimed at developing children's understanding of story structure.

Suitable for

KS1, KS2

Aims

- To sequence events and recount them in appropriate detail.
- To develop the use of a clear structure to organise writing.

Resources

Resources needed will depend on the activity:

- Blank picture books
- DT/craft materials and card
- Paper and pencils

What to do

First, decide between one of these approaches:

1. You could write the stages of the story on cards which are given to the children. They must then decide on the order of the cards.

OR

2. You could ask the children to decide which are the most important moments in the story. These moments are then discussed or written down in the order they occur.

Methods for clarifying story sequence

A. Picture Sequence. The children draw large pictures of the story stages in groups. These pictures are displayed in a timeline on a wall to show the sequence of the story. Alternatively, each group or each child could draw pictures of their own story to show the sequence of events.

B. Picture Book. The children create a picture book by drawing the key events of a story in the correct sequence. You could allow the use of speech bubbles to help explain the events. The books can be made either by folding or stapling.

C. Story Map. The children draw a map of the events in a story from start to finish. Key events can be shown in boxes along the journey. This activity also encourages children to think about the setting.

D. Sequence Card Swap. The children write or draw the sequence of events on separate cards. The sets of cards can then be given to another child or group who has to put them into the correct order.

E. Story Acting. The classroom can be divided up into areas which represent different stages of the story. The children act out the appropriate part of the story in each area.

Broadcast

Broadcast is an exciting activity in which children examine story events from a media perspective. This provides a useful opportunity to develop speaking and listening skills while reinforcing the similarities and differences between written and spoken language.

Suitable for

KS1, KS2

Aims

- To speak competently and creatively for different purposes and audiences.
- To vary actions/writing to suit a purpose.
- To respond imaginatively and engage with texts.

Resources

- Paper and pencils/whiteboards
- Story with which the children are familiar or have been studying
- TV clip of a news broadcast
- Video camera/tape recorder (optional)
- Scenery props, i.e. news desk, story backdrop (optional)

What to do

1. Show the children a TV clip of a news broadcast where a presenter is explaining and commenting on topical events.

2. Lead a discussion on the type of language used by the presenter/news-reader and the information they gave.

3. Remind the children of the story they have been studying, and explain: 'You are going to be making your own news broadcast to tell

the public about the events in the story. You will need to decide which parts of the story are newsworthy and how a news presenter would explain the news. You can work with a partner to create a script for your news broadcast. Once you have written the broadcast, you will need to practise delivering it before you perform it to the rest of class.'

4. Some children may require prompts or frames for their writing which give ideas about suitable language or a summary of newsworthy events from the story.

5. The children perform their news broadcasts, while the others think of constructive comments.

Variations

- The news broadcasts could include interviews with a character from the story, eyewitness accounts or comments from an expert.
- The optional scenery props could be made as part of a linked art/DT project.
- The performances could be recorded using a video camera or tape recorder, and then played back for evaluation.

In Between Scenes

In Between Scenes is an engaging activity which encourages children to explore and develop story characters by creating new or parallel scenes.

Suitable for

KS1, KS2

Aims

- To show an understanding of ideas, events and characters.
- To explore the reasons why things happen, or why characters change/act in a certain way.
- To respond imaginatively and engage with texts.

Resources

- Paper and pencils/whiteboards
- Story with which the children are familiar or have been studying

What to do

1. Lead a discussion on the key events and characters of a story that the children are studying. The plot could be broken down into structural stages such as: beginning, middle, ending *or*
   - Introduction
   - Problem
   - Climax
   - Events
   - Resolution (Suitable for more able children).

2. Highlight an area of the story which occurs in between two of the structural stages, i.e. between the problem and the climax. Explain

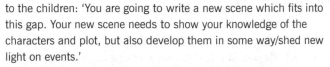

to the children: 'You are going to write a new scene which fits into this gap. Your new scene needs to show your knowledge of the characters and plot, but also develop them in some way/shed new light on events.'

3. The children write their new scene and share their work with a writing partner who reads it carefully and makes constructive criticisms.

Variations

- The new scene which the children write could occur before the actual story begins, after the story ends or run parallel with an existing scene.

Puppet Stories

Puppet Stories is a fun activity which allows children to take on a role in a story. The children will recognise the importance of collaboration and evaluation in terms of their own and others' performances.

Suitable for

KS1, KS2

Aims

- To act out own and well-known stories using voices for characters.
- To respond imaginatively and engage with texts.
- To comment constructively on plays and performances.

Resources

- Puppets to represent story characters (Can be as simple as finger/stick puppets or more elaborate if time allows. This activity works well when linked to a design project on puppet making.)
- Story with which the children are familiar or have been studying (optional)

What to do

1. Lead a discussion about the skills needed to retell a story using puppets. Topics for the discussion could include: using voices for characters, speaking loudly/clearly, co-operation between puppeteers, planning the puppet story, puppet movement, writing of scripts and improvising.

2. Divide the class into groups and allocate a story or section of a story to each group. The children should be encouraged to spend

time initially deciding which characters they will adopt, sharing script ideas and developing details/voices for their puppet characters.

3. The children should then rehearse and refine their puppet stories in preparation for a performance in front of the other groups.

4. When watching the other groups' performances, the children should be encouraged to think of constructive comments which can be shared with the performers.

Variations

- The children could make and wear masks as opposed to using puppets in this activity.
- You can link this activity with Points of View (see page 80) by asking the children to retell the story from a different perspective.
- Try encouraging the children to add new characters to an existing story, or to create a new story involving existing characters.

What Happens Next?

What Happens Next? is an activity in which children improvise ideas about plot and character based on what has already happened in a story. This is a useful opportunity for reinforcing children's knowledge of simple story structure.

Suitable for

KS1, KS2

Aims

- To vary actions/writing to suit a purpose.
- To sustain roles/characters when working with others or individually.
- To develop understanding of genre/text types.

Resources

- Paper and pencils/whiteboards

What to do

1. Stop reading from a story at a key moment and explain: 'You need to think carefully about what might happen next in the story. Take into account: the plot so far, what you know about the characters, and the style/type of writing.'

2. The children can predict what happens next by discussing their ideas with a partner and then writing down their prediction. The children's ideas can then be represented through: drama, discussion, drawing, extended writing or continued/oral storytelling.

3. Once the children have shared their predictions, you can continue reading the story to find out what actually happened next.

Variations

- You could ask older children to give their predictions by stating what will happen in the next story structure stage, i.e.
  1. Introduction
  2. Problem
  3. Climax
  4. Events
  5. Resolution.

Character Conversations

Character Conversations is a fantastic opportunity for children to explore the thoughts and feelings of a character from a story. The aim is to improvise and work in role.

Suitable for

KS2

Aims

* To imagine and explore feelings and ideas.
* To take up and sustain different roles, adapting them to suit the situation.

Resources

* Toy/old telephones (optional)

What to do

1. Lead a discussion about the characters from a chosen text which the children are familiar with. Explain to the children: 'You are going to be working in pairs/groups. You are going to become one of the characters we have discussed and have a conversation with the other characters in your group. You must try to think and talk in the role of your character. Try and ask good questions of the other characters.'

2. You may wish to give the children a specific focus for the conversations, e.g. a situation where a character needs to make an important decision or has a moment of reflection after a significant event.

3. Divide the children into groups, allocate character roles and model a conversation, if necessary, before the activity begins. You could remind the children that they are able to use rumour, speculation and gossip appropriate to their character.

4. A time limit can be set for the conversations. The children can then be asked to share their experiences, or demonstrate some of their conversation to the rest of the class.

Variations

- This activity can be carried out in the form of a telephone conversation between characters. The children communicate news or developments from the story while in role. The character receiving the news should respond appropriately. The telephone conversations can be performed by pairs of children using toy/old telephones in front of the others, who listen in and discuss the conversations at the end.

Character Letters

Character Letters is a stimulating activity which encourages children to show their knowledge of a character from a story. By writing a letter the children can explore the thoughts and feelings of their character, while showing an awareness of the letter's intended recipient.

Suitable for

KS2

Aims

- To imagine and explore feelings and ideas.
- To revise the conventions of letter writing.
- To use language and style appropriate to the reader.

Resources

- Paper and pencils (letter writing templates could be used)
- Story with which the children are familiar or have been studying

What to do

1. Lead a discussion about a character from a chosen text which the children are familiar with. Topics for the discussion could include: reasons why the character has acted as they have, how the character might feel at a particular point in the story, questions which the character may want to ask and opinions held of other characters by the chosen persona.

2. Explain that the children are going to be writing a letter from the chosen story character to another person.

3. There are many options for the recipient of the letter depending on the story being used. Some suggestions for the recipient are: a letter to grandparents, a letter to a pen-pal, a letter to another character in the story.

4. You may need to model the conventions of letter writing and demonstrate how to write as the chosen character.

5. Once the children have completed their letters, they can share them with the rest of the class.

Variations

- Why not extend the activity by allocating writing partners who will write back with a second letter in response to the one written by their partner?
- The activity can be adapted by asking the children to write a diary extract for a character, rather than a letter.

Points of View

Points of View is a challenging activity which requires children to retell a known story from a different point of view from the author's choice of narrator. This gives children the opportunity to imaginatively explore characters' interpretations of events.

Suitable for

KS2

Aims

- To evaluate writers' purposes and viewpoints, and the overall effect of the text on the reader.
- To respond imaginatively and engage with texts.
- To imagine and explore feelings and ideas.

Resources

- Paper and pencils
- Story with which the children are familiar or have been studying

What to do

1. Lead a discussion about the narrator of a chosen story with which the children are familiar. Topics for the discussion could include: reasons why the author may have chosen that character to narrate the story, what effect the choice of narrator has on the story, which other characters would have described the events differently if they were the narrator and how would they have interpreted events differently.

2. Explain that the children are going to be rewriting selected events from a different point of view from the one demonstrated in the story, e.g. writing from the point of view of the donkey in the *Nativity Story* or writing from the point of view of the wolf in *The Three Little Pigs*.

3. You may wish to select specific events which the children must write about from a different point of view, or allow them to choose their own section of the story to reinterpret. You should encourage the children to write imaginatively and take into account the thoughts and feelings of the new narrator.

Variations

- The children could form small groups in which they take turns to retell/reinterpret a stage or event from the story, thus sharing ideas before beginning their individual writing.
- Why not invite the children to retell their new written version of the story to a writing partner?

Chapter 3
Humanities

Geography

History

RE

Humanities

In this section you will find lesson ideas, games and activities for History, Geography and Religious Education. They are grouped together as Humanities here because many of the skills involved are directly transferable between the subjects, and the National Curriculum contains an extensive list of topics to which these skills can be applied.

This section is designed to help develop some of the key skills of the Humanities subjects

- Chronological Awareness
- Historical and Geographical Interpretation and Awareness
- Understanding Environmental Change/Development
- Understanding of Places
- Learning About and From Religion

Orienteering

Orienteering is a fun and practical way to develop key Geography skills while improving fitness. It can be done in the school playground, a field or out in the local environment with the appropriate supervision.

Suitable for

KS1, KS2

Aims

- To use maps and plans including contents, keys and grids.
- To use appropriate geographical vocabulary.

Resources

- Large-scale maps of the orienteering area
- Go to **www.britishorienteering.org.uk** for comprehensive advice and a range of local contacts who will help you to organise events
- Compasses/punches/labels/stakes/pencils (depending on how you organise your orienteering course)

What to do

1. The orienteering course which you create should be tailored to the age and ability of your children. Contact your local development officer through **www.britishorienteering.org.uk** for advice on this, or to find out if there are any existing orienteering courses in your local area.

2. An orienteering course can be created in its simplest form by: drawing a large-scale map of the school environment which includes key fixed features, creating a set of letter cards (these should make a word/phrase when written in the correct order) which need to be attached at various locations in the school environment, and labelling the map with numbers which correspond to the location of the letter cards. Photocopy the map and leave a space for the children to write down the letters which they find at the numbered points on the map.

3. Explain to the children: 'You are going to work in pairs to find out the secret word/phrase hidden on the orienteering course. You will need to use the map to find your way to all the different numbered points; at each number you will find a letter. Write down the letters on your map and arrange them correctly to make the secret word/phrase.'

4. You should start the pairs off at different numbers or at timed intervals to avoid congestion and to avoid pairs following each other rather than following the map.

Variations

- Once the children are familiar with this simple technique you could introduce compasses and directions to the orienteering course.
- Why not turn the activity into a competition, where the fastest pairs receive a prize?
- You could introduce some basic navigation skills by setting up a simple course in the classroom. Use tables and chairs etc. to mark out the course, draw simple symbolic maps and have the children navigate around the course to find objects or letters to make a word.

Take Me There

Take Me There is a great activity in which children develop their awareness of the world. They will choose a country to visit and find out information on their chosen destination.

Suitable for

KS1, KS2

Aims

- To use atlases, globes, maps and plans at a range of scales.
- To draw plans and maps at a range of scales.
- To describe where places are.

Resources

- Atlases/maps (appropriate to ability of the children)
- Internet access (optional)
- Library access (optional)
- Globe (optional)

What to do

1. Divide the class into pairs. Give out an ability appropriate atlas to each partner group. At this point you may need to explain how to use an atlas effectively.

2. Explain to the children: 'You are going to choose a place which you would like to visit, anywhere in the world. It could be a country or a specific place in a country. You need to draw a detailed map of the country, find and label the capital of that country and record any important features on your drawing.'

3. The children could research their chosen location using a library or the internet and make notes on important facts such as population, location, industries, etc.

4. Finally the pairs can present their work to the rest of the class and identify where their location is on a globe or a large world map.

Variations

* Why not use the children's work to contribute towards a 'Where in the World' display (see page 268)?
* You could give the partner groups a continent which they must visit. This can change the next time the activity is done.
* Try setting the children a task such as finding out how far they would have to travel from school to their chosen destination, how long it would take and which countries they would pass through or over.

Environmental Projects

Environmental Projects are a great way to apply geographical skills in a practical cross-curricular way. The children will work in groups to research and take action in school.

Suitable for

KS2

Aims

- To recognise how people may seek to manage environments sustainably, and to identify opportunities for their own involvement.
- To collect and record evidence.
- To analyse evidence and draw conclusions.

Resources

- Computer and internet access
- Poster/leaflet-making materials
- Tape/video recorder (optional)

What to do

1. Divide the class into groups. Hold a discussion to find out what the children know about sustainability, being 'green' and environmental issues.

2. Select some areas for focus for the group projects, i.e. waste, water, electricity, etc. The groups could choose which area they wish to study.

3. Allow the groups to research what happens in school and at home with regard to these issues, i.e. recycling of waste, conservation of water and use of electricity.

4. Instruct/assist the groups to research the global implications of their focus areas. They should find out about the things which can be done to reduce the impact upon the environment caused by their chosen area.

5. The groups can then begin agreeing on recommendations or changes which the school can make to minimise its impact on the environment, i.e. better recycling of waste, ways to save water and methods of using less electricity.

6. Each group can then develop an advertising campaign to promote their cause. This could include making posters, leaflets, websites, and radio or television advertisements.

7. The groups can present their campaign to the whole school in an assembly and introduce new measures such as recycling bins or water and electricity saving measures.

8. Finally the groups can manage and evaluate their projects in terms of the school's impact on the environment.

Variations

- Why not arrange for visitors/experts to come into school to discuss the environmental issues? Your local council and energy providers are useful contacts for this.
- The children can record their project and findings using a multimedia presentation package (Microsoft PowerPoint) which could be presented to the whole school.

Artefact Explorers

Artefact Explorers is an interactive way for children to learn about objects from the past and their uses.

Suitable for

KS1, KS2

Aims

- To find out about events, people and changes from a wide variety of sources (artefacts).
- To identify differences between ways of life at different times.

Resources

- Selection of artefacts (or pictures of artefacts) relevant to history topic being studied
- Artefact Explorer recording sheet/paper/individual whiteboards
- Topic books/internet access (optional)

What to do

1. Divide the class into groups and give out a different artefact to each group. You may wish to explain that the artefact needs to be handled carefully.

2. Explain to the children: 'You are going to be investigating some artefacts in groups and trying to find out as much as you can about them. You will have 30 minutes to answer a series of questions and prepare a presentation about your artefact.'

3. You may wish to suggest areas for the groups to focus on, or you could provide the groups with an Artefact Explorer recording sheet. This sheet could contain the following headings:

- *Draw a picture of the object here . . .*
- *Describe your object here . . .*
- *How do you think it was made?*
- *What is it made from?*
- *Is it damaged or worn away?*
- *What do you think your object was used for?*
- *Are similar objects in use today?*
- *Who do you think might have used it?*
- *Do you think it would have been used every day?*
- *How does the object work?*
- *How has it been decorated?*
- *Do you think it is valuable?*

4. Once each group has completed a presentation, you could reveal the actual purposes and details of the artefacts, discussing whether or not the groups were close to discovering these.

Variations

- Why not allow the groups to use books and the internet to help research their artefact?
- Try approaching your local authority to borrow history project packs which contain artefacts.
- Try contacting local museums to see if they will loan out artefacts to schools.

History Day

> History Day is a great way to learn about different periods of history and develop the notoriously challenging skills of chronological awareness.

Suitable for

KS1, KS2

Aims

- To place events, people and changes into correct periods of time.
- To use dates and vocabulary relating to the passing of time.
- To identify differences between ways of life at different times.

Resources

- Selection of costumes and props (provided by parents if possible)
- Topic books/internet access

What to do

1. Send a letter home to parents explaining that the class (or whole school if appropriate) is going to be having a History Day and that every child needs to come to school dressed as a character from history. The letter should be sent home well in advance to allow preparation time! Encourage the parents to send a reply to school confirming what their child is going to be dressed as, or to ask school for help in preparing a costume for their child.

2. On History Day itself there are many opportunities for learning:

   A. *Human Timeline*. Set the children the task of trying to put themselves into chronological order depending on which historical character they are dressed as.

B. *Clothing Comparisons*. Allow the children to draw each other in their costumes and identify the similarities and differences between themselves.

C. *Character Facts*. Ask the children to use information books and the internet to create a fact file about their historical character.

D. *Diary Entries*. Ask the children to research the lifestyle of their character and write a diary entry for that person.

E. *Timeline Pictures*. Invite the children to draw and cut out a picture of themselves in costume. They can then attach the picture to a timeline in the classroom.

Variations

- Why not play some Hot-Seat games in character (see page 56)?
- You could host an assembly at the end of the day to showcase the costumes and the achievements of the children.
- Try preparing games or food from different periods of history for the children to try out at breaktime.

Time Machine

Time Machine is an excellent idea for teaching children about many aspects of history. The children travel backwards and forwards in time exploring imaginary surroundings, thoughts and feelings. Time Machine provides a useful assessment opportunity.

Suitable for

KS1, KS2

Aims

- To place events, people and changes into correct periods of time.
- To use dates and vocabulary relating to the passing of time.
- To identify differences between ways of life at different times.

Resources

- Time Machine props – time travel control panel
- Time travel sound effects – musical instruments or CD (optional)
- Props/artefacts relevant to the period of history being studied (optional)

What to do

1. Explain to the children: 'Your time travel control panel allows your mind to go backwards or forwards to any point in history or in the future. All you need to do is set the date and time to where you want to go! You might find that you become somebody else from that time with a new name and appearance! When you arrive there I might ask you to act things out, talk to someone or explain your thoughts and appearance'

2. Here are some suggestions for activities using the Time Machine concept:

   A. *Recent History*. Ask the children to set their machines to travel back to one hour ago/24 hours ago/one week ago/one year ago.

   B. *Near Future*. Ask the children to set their machines to travel forward to one hour from now/24 hours from now/one week from now/six months from now, etc.

   C. *100 Years from Now*. Ask the children to travel back or forward 100 years and explain their surroundings, actions, thoughts and appearance. Alternatively, suggest that they have been brought forward or back 100 years to the present time – ask the children what is different.

   D. *Specific Periods*. Use the Time Machine to travel back to a specific period in history to coincide with a topic being studied such as the Tudors, e.g.

      1. Travel back to 1509AD and become Henry VIII – what changes do you want to make to the country? How do you feel?

      2. Travel back to 2400BC and become a slave building the pyramids at Giza – what job are you doing? How do you feel?

   E. *Chronology Assessment*. Invite the children to travel back as far as they can imagine in history. This provides a useful opportunity to assess their level of understanding of chronology.

   F. *Changes*. Tell the children that they can go back in time and make one change. Ask the children to travel forward again and find out what has happened today as a result of the change they made.

Variations

- Why not play some Hot-Seat games in character (see page 56)?
- Try completing some of the time travel activities in pairs or groups where the children can take on different roles.
- You could ask the children to draw or describe what they saw on their travels for an assessment.

Time Travel control panel

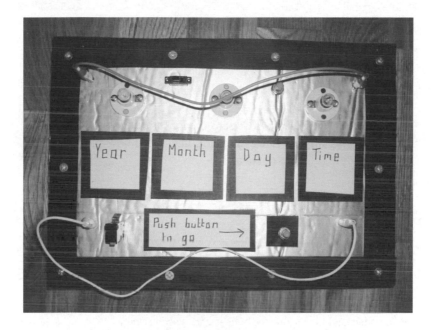

Making the Rules

Making the Rules is a super activity for helping children to understand why we have rules and laws, and how they can help people to make decisions.

Suitable for

KS1, KS2

Aims

- To recognise that religious teachings/rules can make a difference to the way individuals behave.
- To understand the importance of rules and laws in society.

Resources

Extracts from holy/sacred texts on rules or laws

What to do

1. Discuss the topic of rules and laws in religion. You might like to ask some of the following questions: Can you think of any places or people who have rules or laws? Why do religions have rules? What is the difference between a rule and a law? Is it important to follow rules? What happens when you break rules?

2. Share some examples of rules from different holy/sacred texts, e.g. a child-friendly version of the *Ten Commandments* or the *Golden Rule*. Pose the question: Are the rules from holy/sacred texts appropriate today?

3. Explain to the children: 'You are going to be working in groups, creating some rules of your own. Think about the kind of behaviour or actions which you want to encourage. Choose your wording carefully – how will your rules be phrased, i.e. *Don't do this/that or try to be . . .*'

4. Depending on the age and ability of the children you can choose an appropriate rule-making task for them to complete:

   - Make a set of rules for playing tag.
   - Make a set of rules for behaviour in the classroom.
   - Make a set of rules for the whole school.
   - Make a set of rules/laws for a new town.

   When the groups have written their rules they can share them with the rest of the class.

Variations

- The children could help to develop a new set of class/school rules which will be adopted.
- Why not use drama to act out a scene in a classroom with no rules, followed by a classroom with rules?

Quiet Time

Quiet Time is an activity where children get the chance to think about themselves and their own spiritual feelings. It can prove to be an interesting and rewarding experience for all.

Suitable for

KS1, KS2

Aims

- To reflect on and consider religious and spiritual feelings.
- To use senses and have times of quiet reflection.

Resources

- Candle (optional)
- Relaxing music (optional)

What to do

1. Discuss the topics of prayer and reflection with the children. You might like to ask some of the following questions: Why do people pray? Is it important to reflect upon your actions? What is a religious/spiritual feeling? What do people do when praying?

2. Explain to the children: 'We are going to have a quiet time. Make sure you are sitting comfortably. You might find it easier if you close your eyes, or you could focus on the light of the candle (optional). Listen to the calm music and your breathing (optional). I am going to ask you to think about things, and we will have a chance to discuss and share our thoughts at the end.'

3. Once the children are settled you might like to introduce the following ideas/topics/questions:

- What things are you thankful for?
- What makes you happy?
- What makes you sad?
- What can you do to make the world a better place?
- How do you treat others?
- What do others think about you?
- Where is your favourite place?
- How can I be the best person I can be?

4. When the children have finished reflecting on the questions/topics, you could invite them to talk in small groups and share their thoughts and feelings.

Variations

- You could ask the children to write down what they thought about during their quiet time.
- Why not ask the children to create topics/questions for quiet time?

Special Books

Special Books is an effective route for studying the importance of religious/sacred texts. By sharing their own Special Book the children will begin to understand the significance of sacred texts.

Suitable for

KS1, KS2

Aims

* To recognise how and why some texts/stories are sacred in different religions.
* To explore a range of religious stories and sacred writings and talk about their meanings.

Resources

* Special Books (books which the children bring in to school)
* Selection of holy/sacred texts, e.g. Bible/Qur'an/Bhagavad Gita/Guru Granth Sahib
* Special Books recording sheet

What to do

1. Well in advance of the session, ask the children to bring in a book from home which is special to them. This book could be their favourite book from when they were a baby, the first book they were given, their favourite story or a book about a hobby or interest.

2. Discuss with the children why they think books and stories are special, and discuss the meaning of the word 'sacred'.

3. Ask the children to complete a Special Books recording sheet which asks questions about their special book.

4. Choose some children to talk to the class about their special book and the reasons why it is important to them. Alternatively, divide the class into groups, and in each the children take turns to share their special book.

5. Show the children a selection of sacred texts, i.e. Bible (Christianity)/Qur'an (Islam)/Bhagavad Gita (Hinduism)/Guru Granth Sahib (Sikhism). Discuss how the sacred books should be treated and the reasons why people might look to a sacred text for guidance.

6. Read a passage from one or more of the sacred texts and discuss how they could be useful to someone needing guidance. (Sacred text translations are readily available on the internet.)

Variations

- Ask the children to write a story for an extension activity which would give advice or guidance to someone about an important issue.
- You could allow groups to research the sacred texts from various religions, collate this information and create a Special Books display.
- Why not invite visitors from local faith communities to share their thoughts on their sacred text?

Special Books Recording Sheet

L.O. - To understand why books can be special to people.

Name: Harry Bond   Date: 25.6.08

SPECIAL BOOKS

*What is the title of your special book?

The Bad Beginning

*Who is the author of your special book?

Lemony Snicket

*Why is your book special to you?

This book is really good because it has got a happy ending at the end of the story.

*Draw the cover of the book here:

*Share your work and talk about your book with two other people on your table.

Chapter 4
Mathematics

Mathematics

In this section you will find lesson ideas, games and activities which aim to develop children's number, shape, space, measuring and handling data skills.

Many of the ideas have a physical (kinaesthetic) element, and there are lots of exciting activities to help stimulate children in Mathematics/Numeracy lessons.

Nearly all of the activities are adaptable to use as a mental/oral starter, or extendable to use as a main lesson activity.

Some of the activities make use of standard classroom mathematics equipment such as a counting stick or digit cards, while others can be taught without resources.

Mathematics tip

If the children have done some mathematics work on an individual whiteboard and you would like to keep it as evidence, photocopy it before erasing it.

Archery

Archery is a fun game in which a child gets to shoot imaginary arrows at a target. The other children then have to work out what the score for that archer would be.

Suitable for

KS1, KS2

Aims

- To improve addition of 1, 2 or 3 digit numbers.
- To develop addition of decimals or fractions.
- To use a calculator for calculations involving several digits.

Resources

- Archery target to be drawn or displayed on whiteboard
- Class set of individual whiteboards and pens
- Whiteboard pen for the archer
- Number fans/number arrow cards (optional)
- Toy archery bow, but no arrows (optional)!

What to do

1. The children should sit at their desks or facing the board, with a space left for one child to stand with a clear line of sight towards the board.

2. Explain to the children: 'I am going to choose one person at a time to be the archer. They will hold the bow (optional) and fire three imaginary arrows at the target; after they have fired each arrow they will say the number on which their arrow landed and mark the number with a dot on the target. Your job is to work out the

archer's total score and write it down on your whiteboard. I will choose the next archer from those of you who work out the total score correctly.'

3. Wipe off the arrow marks. The next archer takes over once the correct total has been established.

Variations

- Change the values on the archery target to make the game easier or more difficult. You can also increase or decrease the number of arrows the archer fires.
- You could set a total score which you want the archer to achieve with their arrows. The other children add the numbers to see if the desired total was reached.
- You could invite individual children to explain the method which they used to calculate the total and explore alternative ways of counting.
- The numbers on the target can be replaced with decimals or fractions.
- The total scored could be shown using number fans or number arrow cards rather than on whiteboards.
- The activity can be extended by creating worksheets with differentiated targets for the children to add arrow marks to and calculate the totals.
- Why not invite the children to add the individual scores or whole class scores using a calculator?

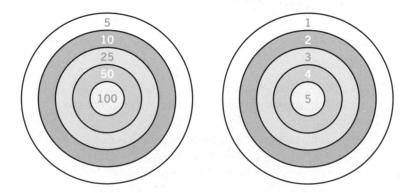

Templates for these images are available to download from the companion website. at www.pearsoned.co.uk/barron

Bingo

Bingo is a versatile and enjoyable game which can be used to teach and assess many aspects of number work/calculation. The children choose their numbers, tick off their answers and shout 'Bingo' to win the game.

Suitable for

KS1, KS2

Aims

● To improve mental addition or subtraction of 1, 2 or 3 digit numbers.
● To consolidate knowledge of multiplication or division facts.

Resources

● Whiteboard/flipchart and pens for the teacher
● Class set of individual whiteboards and pens/exercise books

What to do

1. Explain to the children: 'We are going to play Bingo. I am going to write 10 numbers up on the board/chart. You need to choose any five of these numbers and write them down. The numbers which are on the board will be the answers to some addition questions which I am going to ask. When one of your numbers is the answer to a question, you should cross it out or circle it. If all five of your numbers are used up then you have won and you need to shout "Bingo."'

2. To begin with you may wish to discuss the answer to each question as the game progresses to ensure that the children don't miss any of their numbers. As they become more confident, you

can just call out the questions and the children will be left to calculate the answer and mark off their numbers where appropriate.

3. You might like to check the winners' Bingo numbers by calling out the questions again and asking the winners to give the answers.

Variations

- You could try asking a mixture of questions using different operations in the same game.
- You could invite able children to be the Bingo caller and create questions to give the Bingo answers.
- Why not try playing Bingo with decimals or fractions?
- You can differentiate the questions to make sure that all children are able to calculate some of the answers and mark off their numbers.

Build a Wall

Build a Wall is a practical activity which reinforces children's knowledge of fractions by asking the whole class to help in the construction of a fraction wall.

Suitable for

KS1, KS2

Aims

- To understand unit fractions and fractions that are several parts of a whole.
- To understand simple equivalent fractions.

Resources

- Large complete fraction wall (fractions included will depend upon ability of children)
- Fraction wall divided up into bricks/pieces
- Blu-Tack
- Whiteboard placed at a reachable height for children

What to do

1. Give out all of the bricks/pieces of the fraction wall to the children equally; the bricks/pieces need to have a piece of Blu-Tack attached. You can then refer the children to a complete fraction wall and discuss it.

2. Ask the children: 'Who is holding the 1 whole unit brick/piece?' This child comes forward and attaches the 1 whole unit brick to the top of the whiteboard. Remind the children about unit fractions, e.g. $\frac{1}{2}$, $\frac{1}{4}$, and fractions that are several parts of one whole, e.g. $\frac{2}{4}$, $\frac{2}{3}$.

3. Explain to the children: 'We are going to take turns to add a brick to the fraction wall in the correct place. When you come to the board, you need to check if a row of bricks has been started with your fraction on it. If so, you add your brick to the end of that row. If not, then start a new row underneath the last one. When you attach your brick you need to say what fraction is now present in your row, i.e. "two thirds", if you attach the second brick which has a value of one third.'

4. The children add their bricks to the fraction wall until the wall is completed.

Variations

- Why not ask the children to identify any equivalent fractions which become obvious when they attach their brick to the wall? These equivalent fractions can be listed on the whiteboard.
- The same task can be given to smaller groups of children with their own fraction bricks. One group could be given halves, quarters, eighths and sixteenths, while the other group is given thirds, sixths, ninths and twelfths. The results can then be displayed together for comparison.
- This activity can be followed up by asking children to answer questions using individual fraction walls. The questions could be about: comparing fractions, equivalent fractions or ordering fractions.

Fraction Wall example

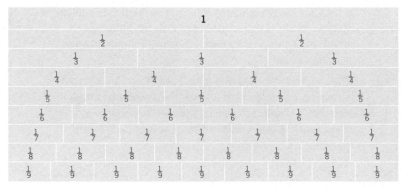

Compass Jumps

Compass Jumps is a fun and active game which can be used to teach children about direction, right angles and compass points.

Suitable for

KS1, KS2

Aims

- To recognise the four compass points.
- To recognise right angles.
- To develop an understanding of clockwise and anticlockwise direction.

Resources

- Compass (optional)
- North, South, East, West cards (optional)

What to do

1. Invite the children to stand in a space, all facing in the same direction.
2. Explain to the children: 'We are going to be jumping to face a compass point of North (N), South (S), East (E) or West (W). If we face the whiteboard, we are facing North. If we turn and face in the opposite direction, we will be facing South. From facing North, if we turn one right angle (90 degrees) clockwise, we will be facing East. If we face East, and turn in the opposite direction, we will be facing West. I am going to shout out a compass point: you need to turn and face that compass point.'

3. Shout out the compass points to take the children around in a clockwise direction, i.e. N, E, S, W, followed by moving in an anticlockwise direction, i.e. N, W, S, E, then you can shout out directions in any order until the children are familiar with points.

Variations

- You could display a large compass point card on the appropriate wall/window, i.e. 'NORTH'. This indicates which direction the class is facing. These can be removed once the children are confident.
- Why not use a magnetic compass initially to work out with the children which direction North actually is, and then highlight the other compass points? Alternatively, describe the front of the class as North.
- The number of compass points can be increased to eight, i.e. N, NE, E, SE, S, SW, W, and NW. The children can jump to face these directions.
- You could introduce directions before stating the compass point to jump to, i.e. 'Turn clockwise to face South' or 'Turn anticlockwise to face East.'
- Try using right angles as commands, i.e. 'Turn one right angle clockwise from North" or "Turn three right angles anticlockwise from South.'
- Try using degrees as commands, i.e. 'Turn 90 degrees clockwise from North' or 'Turn 180 degrees anticlockwise from South.'
- Why not ask a child to take over the role of calling out the compass points or instructions?

Compass Point cards example

N NORTH	S SOUTH
E EAST	W WEST

Counting Actions

Counting Actions is a great physical and mental maths warm-up activity. The children need to count up or back in the appropriate steps while carrying out the correct action.

Suitable for

KS1, KS2

Aims

- To develop the skills of counting on or back from any number in a range of steps.
- To reinforce times tables knowledge and understanding of patterns.
- To identify odd and even numbers.

Resources

- Large number square/multiplication square (optional)

What to do

1. Have the children sit in a circle; this is optional, but will make the game easier for younger children to follow.

2. Explain to the children: 'We are going to be counting on in steps of ten, starting at zero. We are going to be doing actions while we count. When we say the first number we will tap our knees, when we say the next number we will clap, then, on the next number we will tap our knees. We are going to count together up to 100.'

3. Ask the children to count back to zero while repeating the knee tap and clap action pattern.

4. When they are used to this, you can change the size of the steps, and change the counting actions to include hands on heads, shoulders, knees or toes, finger clicks or waving.

Variations

- You can write the numbers needed for the sequence on the whiteboard until the children are confident. Alternatively, you could refer the children to a number square or multiplication table to identify the steps and patterns.
- Why not ask the children to identify odd numbers in a sequence with a clap, and even numbers with a knee tap? This can be done while the children count in steps of any size, and should be discussed afterwards to reveal any odd/even patterns in the sequence.
- The starting number can be replaced with a decimal or fraction.
- Ask the children to predict which action will be done on the last number of the sequence, and to explain the reason for their choice.

Counting Stick Games

A Counting Stick is a versatile maths resource. The children learn to count up or back in the appropriate steps from any integer. The counting stick can be used to introduce concepts such as negative numbers, estimating and visualisation.

Suitable for

KS1, KS2

Aims

- To improve the skills of counting on or back from any number in a range of steps.
- To encourage visualisation of number sequences.
- To develop approximating and estimating with distance and number.

Resources

- Counting stick with coloured divisions
- Digit cards and Blu-Tack

What to do

1. The children need to sit facing you at a short distance. The following games can be played in any order, and can be selected to deliver a particular learning objective.
2. Hold the counting stick in one hand, leaving the other hand free to point, using a finger or pencil, to different parts of the counting stick.

Follow Me

Show the children the counting stick and explain: 'The stick begins at zero and ends at ten. I am going to be pointing to different parts of the counting stick; you need to say which number I am pointing to.'

There are key questions which can be asked in most of the Counting Stick Games before they begin: 'What value will it be if I point to the beginning/middle/end of the stick? What is each section worth?'

Begin by counting up the stick from zero to ten, then back from ten to zero. You can then jump in intervals from one number to any other on the counting stick and the children say the numbers that are indicated, i.e. 2/7/10/0/5.

You should choose appropriate values for the beginning and end of the stick depending on the children's ability.

Sticky Numbers (Suitable for younger children)

Show the children the counting stick and explain: 'I am going to give out some digit cards with a piece of Blu-Tack on the back. We are going to take turns to attach the cards in the correct place on the counting stick. The counting stick begins at zero and ends at ten.'

Once the digit cards have been attached correctly, lead the children in counting up and down the stick. You should create number cards to use in this activity which are appropriate to the children's level of ability.

Mysterious Stick

Show the children the counting stick and explain: 'I am going to tell you the value of one part of the counting stick. Your job is to work out what the values of the other parts will be. If the middle of the stick is 40, what could the beginning and end be?'

Encourage the children to give answers which are an equal distance apart, i.e. 30 and 50, 20 and 60, or 35 and 45. Then you can test their suggested numbers by counting up and down the stick in the appropriate divisions. Choose appropriate values for the middle of the stick depending on the pupil's ability.

Endless Stick

This game develops visualisation skills. Show the children the counting stick and explain: 'The counting stick begins at 0 and ends at 100. Where would 150 be?' Invite a child to indicate where the 150 point would be *if* the counting stick continued.

Similarly, you could explain: 'The counting stick begins at 80 and ends at 180. Where would 40 be?' Choose appropriate values for the beginning and end of the stick depending on the children's ability.

Variations

- Why not ask a child to take the role of leader in any of these Counting Stick Games?
- The Counting Stick games can be extended for more able children by using decimals or fractions as the values, or counting back into negative numbers.

Function Machine

Function Machine is an extremely useful and versatile activity. It can be used to teach, practise or assess many different numeracy skills. The children have to calculate what happens when a number travels through the function machine.

Suitable for

KS1, KS2

Aims

- To develop knowledge of doubling and halving numbers.
- To develop addition/subtraction/multiplication/division skills.
- To develop counting on or back from any number.

Resources

- Function Machine to be drawn or displayed on whiteboard
- Class set of individual whiteboards and pens
- Number fans/number arrow cards (optional)
- Calculators

What to do

1. Draw or display the Function Machine on the board and highlight the 'IN,' 'OUT' and 'Function' areas of the machine.

2. Explain to the children: 'This is a function machine. Numbers go into the machine where it says "IN," the number gets changed according to what the function is set to, then the new number will come out of the machine where it says "OUT." For example, if the machine is set to double numbers [x 2 is drawn on the machine], then if the number 10 was put into the machine, the number 20 would come out. You need to calculate the number which would come out of the machine and write it down on your whiteboard.'

3. Choose a series of numbers to put into the machine and the children work through them discussing how they calculated the answer.

Variations

- Change the function on the machine to focus on a different operation/calculation.
- Ask a child to suggest numbers to put into the Function Machine. They can predict the outcome while the others calculate the answer and write it on their whiteboards.
- The numbers going into the Function Machine can be replaced with decimals or fractions.
- The activity can be extended by creating worksheets containing differentiated Function Machines.
- Why not ask the children to explore the inverse operation to the calculations by working out what would happen if the numbers were to go through the machine in reverse, i.e. the number goes into the 'OUT' side and appears at the 'IN' side?
- You could allow the children to use calculators to work out the answers.
- The children could show their answers using number fans or arrow cards.
- Why not encourage younger children to make machine noises as the number travels through the Function Machine?

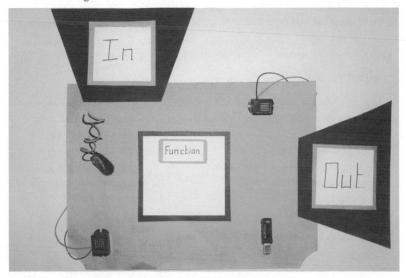

Guess my Number

Guess my Number is a simple game in which children take turns to ask closed questions with the goal of discovering the number the leader is thinking of.

Suitable for

KS1, KS2

Aims

- To develop reasoning and logical thinking skills.
- To reinforce knowledge of key concepts such as odd and even numbers, multiples, etc.
- To develop the use of precise mathematical language.
- To ask appropriate mathematical questions.

Resources

- Whiteboard and pen for leader
- Class set of whiteboards and pens (optional)

What to do

1. Explain to the children: 'I am going to think of a number. Your job is to work out which number I am thinking of. You are going to take turns to ask questions to which I can only answer "Yes" or "No". You need to listen carefully to all of the questions and answers if you are going to guess the number correctly. Do not try to guess the actual number until you are reasonably sure. You are only going to be allowed to ask 20 questions. If you have not guessed the number correctly after 20 questions, then I have won!'

2. You may wish to give some examples of appropriate closed questions, i.e.: 'Is the number odd? Is the number below 50? Is the number a multiple of five? Is the number between 20 and 30?'

3. Once the game begins, you can keep a tally of the number of questions asked on the whiteboard. The children could either be asked to raise their hands if they want to ask a question, or they could take turns to ask one question per person/table group.

4. Once the number has been guessed correctly, you could draw attention to any particularly good questions which were asked, and repeat the game using a different number.

Variations

- Why not change the number of questions the children are allowed to ask? Reducing the number will promote very careful thinking and discourage wasted questions.
- You could ask a confident child to choose a number and lead the game. It may be advisable to have the child share their number with you to begin with.
- The numbers chosen can be replaced with decimals or fractions.
- You could make a brief note of each question asked on the whiteboard; the answers can also be recorded to help children to remember the previous stages of the game. Alternatively, the children can keep a record of the questions and answers on their own whiteboards.

Guess my Shape

Guess my Shape is a great game in which children take turns to ask closed questions with the goal of discovering the shape the leader is hiding.

Suitable for

KS1, KS2

Aims

- To visualise and describe 2D shapes.
- To understand the properties of 2D shapes.
- To develop the use of precise mathematical language.
- To ask appropriate mathematical questions.
- To develop reasoning and logical thinking skills.

Resources

- Selection of 2D shapes
- Shape cards (optional)
- Whiteboard and pen for leader
- Class set of whiteboards and pens (optional)

What to do

1. Explain to the children: 'I am going to hide a 2D shape. Your job is to work out which shape I have hidden. You are going to take turns to ask questions to which I can only answer "Yes" or "No". You need to listen carefully to all of the questions and answers if you are going to guess the shape correctly. Do not try to guess the actual shape until you are reasonably sure. You are only going to be allowed to ask five questions. If you have not guessed the shape correctly after five questions, then I have won!'

2. You may wish to give some examples of appropriate closed questions, i.e.: 'Is the shape regular? Does the shape have any right angles? Does the shape have more than three sides?'

3. Once the game begins, you could keep a tally of the number of questions asked on the whiteboard.

4. Once the shape has been guessed correctly, you can reveal the shape and draw attention to any particularly good questions which were asked. The game is then repeated using a different shape.

Variations

- You can change the number of questions the children are allowed to ask. Reducing the number will promote very careful thinking and discourage wasted questions.
- Why not ask a confident child to choose a shape and lead the game? It may be advisable to have the child share their shape with you to begin with.
- Try giving less able children a selection of 2D shapes to help them eliminate shapes after a question has been asked. Alternatively, a set of cards with drawings of the 2D shapes could be used. Shape cards could be given to every child if necessary, and they can be held up by the children to show which shape they believe you are hiding.
- A variation of this game is to allow the children to see a small section of the shape, such as a corner, before the questions are asked. The shape should be held behind a screen and the small section can 'peep' over the top.
- Why not extend the game by using 3D shapes in the same way?

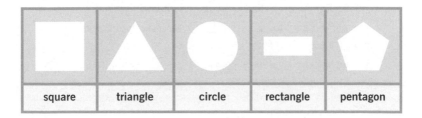

| square | triangle | circle | rectangle | pentagon |

Missing Numbers

Missing Numbers is an activity which encourages children to create lists of possible calculations for a given answer. Missing Numbers can be used for reinforcing knowledge of addition, subtraction, multiplication and division.

Suitable for

KS1, KS2

Aims

- To develop understanding of the four number operations and the relationship between them.
- To find possible missing numbers in calculations.

Resources

- Whiteboard and pen for leader
- Class set of whiteboards and pens
- Sand timer (optional)

What to do

1. Explain to the children: 'I am going to write a calculation on the whiteboard. There will be significant parts of the calculation missing. You need to list as many ways as you can of making it into a correct calculation.'

2. Give an example question such as __ × __ = 20, then list some, or all, of the correct permutations on the board, i.e. $5 \times 4 = 20/10 \times 2 = 20/20 \times 1 = 20$.

3. Then write a new missing number problem. The children can be given a time limit in which they have to list as many permutations as they can. (A sand timer is a useful tool for this purpose.)

4. Once the time limit has expired, ask the children to give their solutions, which can be recorded on the whiteboard.

Variations

- Why not give differentiated problems using different operations for the children to solve, e.g. __ + __ = 20 (for lower ability group) and __ × __ = 160 (for higher ability)?
- The activity can be extended by setting the children a mixture of Missing Numbers problems to solve.

Missing Sequence

Missing Sequence is a fun game which encourages children to listen carefully to spot a missing number in a sequence. The game can be used to reinforce and assess understanding of several mathematical concepts such as multiples, prime numbers and number patterns.

Suitable for

KS1, KS2

Aims

- To recognise and describe number patterns.
- To make predictions and general statements about numbers.

Resources

- Whiteboard and pen for leader
- Class set of whiteboards and pens
- Sand timer (optional)

What to do

1. Explain to the children: 'I am going to say a sequence of numbers. There will be a number missing from the sequence. You need to work out the missing number and write it down on your whiteboard. It might help if you write down the number sequence as I say it.'

2. Give an example of a missing sequence such as: '2,4,6,8,10,**,14,16,18,20.' The missing number '12' can be revealed. Explain the reasons why this was the missing number.

3. Reveal a new Missing Sequence problem. The children can be given a time limit in which they have to discover the missing number. (A sand timer is a useful tool for this purpose.) When the children have found the missing number, they should prepare an explanation using good mathematical vocabulary, and look for any patterns in the sequence.

4. Once the time limit has expired, you can ask the children to give their solution, explanation and share any patterns they spotted.

Variations

- You could try missing out more than one number from the sequence.
- Why not ask the children to continue the sequence with five more numbers?
- The activity can be extended by setting the children a selection of differentiated Missing Sequence problems.

Number Shapes

Number Shapes is a useful mental maths starter which encourages children to use a range of mental addition and subtraction methods to find a total or a missing number.

Suitable for

KS1, KS2

Aims

- To develop addition methods for three or more one or two digit numbers.
- To find the missing number in calculations.
- To calculate a number by finding the difference.
- To reinforce knowledge of 2D shape properties.

Resources

- Whiteboard and pen for leader
- Class set of whiteboards and pens (optional)

What to do

1. Explain to the children: 'I am going to draw a shape on the whiteboard. I will write a number in each corner of the shape. I will write the total of these numbers from the corners in the middle of the shape.'

2. Draw a triangle as an example on the board, and then write the numbers: 5, 12 and 20 in the corners. Discuss how to add these numbers together using methods appropriate to the children's ability, and write the total of 37 in the middle of the shape.

3. The numbers in the triangle can be changed and the children can calculate the new total and write it down on their whiteboards. You

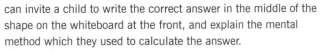

can invite a child to write the correct answer in the middle of the shape on the whiteboard at the front, and explain the mental method which they used to calculate the answer.

4. You can continue to set similar Number Shape problems, or use a different shape such as a square or pentagon.

Variations

- Change the focus of the game by writing a total in the middle of the shape at the beginning, and leaving out one or more of the corner numbers for the children to calculate.
- The game can be extended into a main lesson activity by setting the children a mixture of Number Shapes problems to solve individually.

Number Tennis

Number Tennis is an active game which children will enjoy. Two teams bat an imaginary tennis ball back and forth while shouting out a number.

Suitable for

KS1, KS2

Aims

- To develop counting on or back in units, tens, hundreds or thousands from one, two, three or four digit numbers.

Resources

- Length of rope/string/display border paper to mark out a net line between the two teams
- Large number square and multiplication square (optional)

What to do

1. Invite the children to sit in two mixed-ability teams which face each other on either side of a net line which is marked with a length of string, rope or display border paper.

2. Explain to the children: 'Pick up your imaginary tennis racquet, I am holding the imaginary tennis ball! When your team hits the ball you have to say the correct number in the sequence. The ball will then be hit by the other team who will say the next number in the sequence as they hit it. For example, if the rule was "Count up in tens from the number 10", then the team I give the imaginary ball to (team A) would start off by serving the ball and saying "10". The other team (team B) would then say "20" as they hit the ball.

Team A would then say "30" as they hit the ball. I will tell you when the game is finished. You all need to work as a team by saying the correct number together and watching the ball as it flies through the air!'

3. You can stop the game/rally at any point if the majority of the team get their number wrong. Once the children have mastered a sequence, you can change the starting point or introduce a new rule.

Variations

- Why not ask the children to count back in the same way from the point at which the game/rally is stopped? Alternatively, a stopping point number can be set before the rally begins; at this point the children will start counting back straight away.
- You could ask individuals or pairs of children to stand up and represent their team. The game is played in the same way, but you will have the opportunity to assess the specific children involved.
- You may wish to write up the sequence of numbers and discuss the rule before the children play the first game. Similarly, a number square or multiplication square can be referred to if appropriate.
- The game can also be played using fractions or decimals.

Treasure Hunter

Treasure Hunter is a fun game which teaches children about direction, movement and compass points. The children will need to give clear and precise instructions if they are to successfully navigate their way to the treasure.

Suitable for

KS1, KS2

Aims

- To recognise and use the four compass points.
- To understand direction.
- To give clear and accurate instructions.

Resources

- North, South, East, West cards
- Treasure (e.g. stickers/sweets or healthy snacks/tokens for Golden Time)

What to do

1. Have the children sit facing in the same direction. Display four compass point cards on the walls or windows of the classroom: North (N), South (S), East (E) and West (W).

2. Explain to the children: 'I am going to place some treasure somewhere in the classroom. One person will be the treasure hunter, and the other children will be the navigators. The navigators will take turns to give one instruction at a time to the treasure hunter. The instructions can include a compass point and a number of steps, e.g. "Move five steps North" or "Move four

steps East." The treasure hunter has to move around objects, not over or under them.'

3. Place some treasure in the classroom and choose children to take turns at being the navigator. Once the treasure is found, a new treasure hunter can be chosen.

Variations

- Once the children are confident with the game and compass points, the compass point cards can be taken down.
- You could choose one child to be the navigator and give all of the instructions to the treasure hunter.
- The game can be extended by limiting the number of instructions which the navigator is allowed to give to the treasure hunter. The number of instructions used can be recorded in a tally chart. This encourages the children to find the shortest route to the treasure. If the treasure hunter doesn't reach the treasure once all of the instructions are used up, then the treasure belongs to the teacher.
- The number of compass points used can be increased to eight, i.e. N, NE, E, SE, S, SW, W, and NW.
- The children can draw a birds-eye representation of the classroom. Mark the position of some treasure, draw an appropriate route from the start point to the treasure and record the instructions needed in a list.
- The treasure hunter could be asked to leave the room while the teacher hides the treasure.

Grid Problem

Grid Problem is a stimulating activity to use as a maths warm-up. The children will need to use logical thinking and reasoning to work out the multiplication question. The children will need to be familiar with the grid method of multiplication before attempting this activity.

Suitable for

KS2

Aims

- To reinforce understanding of multiplication grids.
- To develop logical thinking skills.
- To develop reasoning skills.
- To solve problems using trial and error.

Resources

- Multiplication Grid – either drawn or displayed on a whiteboard
- Class set of whiteboards and pens

What to do

1. Display a multiplication grid with the numbers inside filled in, but no calculation (see example below).

2. Explain to the children: 'You need to work out what the multiplication calculation would have been to make this grid. Once you have worked it out, you need to write down the full number sentence/calculation on your whiteboard.'

3. There are only two multiples of ten that multiply to make 100. You may need to draw attention to this. Once this is established then the remaining calculations can be completed quickly.

4. Once the children have written down their answers, you can choose a pupil to come to the board and fill in the gaps in the grid, to test and write down the calculation. (14 × 12 = 168)

×		
	100	40
	20	8

×	10	4
10	100	40
2	20	8

14 × 12 = 168

Variations

- You can choose to reduce or increase the number of elements missed out of the grid problems.
- Why not allow the children to create a grid problem for a partner to solve by exchanging whiteboards and then checking answers?

Guess my Rule

Guess my Rule is a great mental maths starter. The children need to choose a number to help guess the rule. The game requires the children to use and apply their mathematical knowledge.

Suitable for

KS2

Aims

- To develop reasoning and logical thinking skills.
- To identify patterns and present solutions.
- To reinforce knowledge of key concepts such as multiples, rounding, odd and even numbers, etc.

Resources

- Whiteboard with YES/NO grid displayed or drawn on it

What to do

1. Explain to the children: 'I will think of a rule, but I will keep it a secret (e.g. odd numbers, multiples of five, numbers which round to 40, prime numbers). I will ask those who have their hand up to tell me a number. If that number fits my rule, I will write it in the YES column. If that number doesn't fit my rule, I will write it in the NO column. Once we have had ten answers, I will allow you to guess my rule; but make sure that you have tested your rule idea with the numbers in the YES and NO columns.'

2. Once the rule has been established, there can be a discussion about what the rule was and how the children worked it out.

3. The activity is then repeated using a new rule.

Variations

- Why not ask a confident child to choose a rule and lead the game? It may be advisable to have them share their rule with you to begin with.
- Guess My Rule can be extended by giving the children differentiated problems to solve. The children will need to write down the rule for sets of numbers, or write down lists of numbers which fit a particular rule.

Standing Rule

Standing Rule is an ideal mental maths starter. The children who choose a number which fits the rule are invited to stand at the front. The game requires the children to use and apply their mathematical knowledge.

Suitable for

KS2

Aims

- To develop reasoning and logical thinking skills.
- To identify patterns and present solutions.
- To reinforce knowledge of key concepts such as multiples, rounding, odd and even numbers, etc.

Resources

- Class set of individual whiteboards and pens

What to do

1. Children sit facing the board, with a space left at the front of the class for children to stand in when they have chosen an appropriate answer.

2. Explain to the children: 'You will need to write a number below 50 on your whiteboard. I will think of a rule, but I will keep it a secret (e.g. odd numbers, multiples of five, numbers which round to 40, prime numbers). I will invite anybody whose number fits my rule to come and stand at the front and show their whiteboard to the others. You can change the number on your whiteboard until you find one which fits my rule.'

3. You can choose whether the children are allowed to repeat numbers that are already present at the front.

4. Once most or all of the children have a number which fits the rule, there can be a discussion about what the rule was and how the children worked it out.

5. The children return to their seats and a new game begins.

Variations

- Try asking a child to choose a rule and lead the game. It may be advisable to have them share their rule with you to begin with.
- Standing Rule can be extended by giving the children differentiated problems to solve, requiring them to write down the rule for sets of numbers, or write down lists of numbers which fit a particular rule.

What's Happening?

What's Happening is a useful mental maths game. The children suggest numbers which change according to a secret rule. The challenge is to work out what the secret rule is. The game requires the children to use and apply their mathematical knowledge (Ma1).

Suitable for

KS2

Aims

- To develop reasoning and logical thinking skills.
- To identify patterns and present solutions.
- To draw conclusions from information.

Resources

- Whiteboard with 'What's Happening' grid displayed or drawn on it

What to do

1. Explain to the children: 'I will think of a rule, but I will keep it a secret (e.g. double the number/add three/take away seven/multiply by five/multiply by three then take away two). You will take turns to tell me a number which I will write down in the column called "YOUR NUMBER". I will do something to the number according to my rule and then write down the new number in the "MY ANSWER" column. Once we have had five numbers, I will allow you to guess my rule; but make sure that you have tested your rule idea with the numbers on the "What's Happening" grid.'

2. Once the rule has been established, there can be a discussion about what the rule was and how the children worked it out.

3. The game starts again with the creation of a new secret rule and renewing the 'What's Happening' grid.

Variations

- Try asking a child to choose a rule and lead the game. It may be advisable to have them share their rule with you to begin with.
- You can increase or reduce the amount of numbers given before the children are allowed to guess the rule.
- What's Happening can be extended by giving the children differentiated problems to solve individually. Completed grids can be supplied for the children to work out the rule, or the rule can be supplied with a blank grid for the children to complete.

What's Happening? grid example

Your Number	My Answer
2	6
11	33
7	21
6	18
25	75

The rule was: × 3

Chapter 5
Music

Music

In the Music section you will find great ideas to develop children's performing, composing and appraising skills.

Music is traditionally a subject which some non-specialist teachers find challenging. The activities contained in this section are simply explained and accessible for a non-specialist teacher. However, if there are any words which you are unsure about then have a look at the helpful Music Glossary (see page 147).

It is advisable to develop a set of Music Golden Rules before beginning any of the instrument-based activities. Ideally the rules should be made and agreed with the children.

Here are some suggestions for Music Golden Rules:

Music Golden Rules

- Stop when you hear the stop sound *or*
- Stop when you see the red card.
- Treat the instruments with respect.
- Do not play when the teacher is talking.

Music Glossary

Allegro	Lively, fast.
Beat	A pulse (every tick on a metronome is a beat).
Chord	Three or four notes played simultaneously.
Conductor	Someone who directs a group of performers.
Crescendo	Becoming gradually louder.
Duet	A piece of music for two players or singers.
Dynamics	The loudness or softness of a piece of music.
Flat	A symbol which shows the note is diminished by one semitone.
Forte	Play loud.
Interval	The distance in pitch between two notes.
Introduction	The opening section of a piece of music.
Key Signature	The flats and sharps at the beginning of a line of music.
Major	One of the two modes of the tonal system. Music written in major keys has a positive/happy sound.
Measure	Where the beats on the lines of the staff are divided up into two, three or four beats to a measure.
Minor	One of the two modes of the tonal system. Music written in minor keys has a dark/sad sound.
Natural	A symbol which means that a note returns to its original pitch.
Note	A pitched sound.
Octave	Eight full tones above a key note that a scale began on.
Orchestra	A large group of instruments playing together.
Pentatonic	A musical scale with five notes.
Percussion Instrument	An object which produces a sound by being hit with an implement, shaken, rubbed, scraped, or by any other action which sets the object into vibration.
Phrase	A single line of music, played or sung.
Piano	An instruction in sheet music to play softly.
Pitch	How high or low a note sounds.

Pizzicato	String instruments plucked instead of bowed.
Presto	Fast.
Rhythm	The controlled movement of music in time.
Score	A piece of music written down in notes.
Sharp	A symbol which shows the note is to be raised by one semitone.
Staff	Where notes are written – made up of five lines and the spaces between them.
Tempo	The speed of a piece of music.
Timbre	Tone colour or quality of sound that distinguishes one instrument from another.
Time Signature	A numeric symbol which shows the number of beats to a measure.
Unison	Two or more voices or instruments playing the same note simultaneously.

Body Sounds

Body Sounds is a fun game to help children learn about performing to a regular beat. The children use their bodies to make music; they will need to watch carefully to keep up!

Suitable for

KS1

Aims

- To rehearse and perform with others, e.g. starting and finishing together, keeping to a steady pulse.
- To learn how sounds can be made in different ways.

Resources

- Untuned percussion instruments (optional)

What to do

1. The children form a circle and you explain: 'We are going to be making music with our bodies! You need to watch carefully, copying exactly what I do.'

2. Clap four beats out slowly and count out each beat as 1, 2, 3, 4. Repeat several times. Then continue counting, but change the action from clapping to clicking.

3. The children join in, copying you as you change between clapping and clicking while counting out 1, 2, 3, 4.

4. When the class is used to this, you could change the actions more quickly, increasing in difficulty as the game progresses. You could try using knee taps (uncrossed and crossed arms), elbow taps or marching.

Variations

- You could choose an able child to take control of the game and lead the actions; this allows you to carefully observe the other children's progress.
- The children could be split into two groups. One group act as timekeepers by playing a beat on 1, 2, 3, 4, using a percussion instrument, while the other group perform body sounds and follow the leader. These groups can then swap roles.

Metal vs. Wood

Metal vs. Wood is a simple game for teaching children about different types of percussion instruments and the sounds they make.

Suitable for

KS1

Aims

* To develop knowledge of percussion instruments.
* To explore the sounds made by different instruments.

Resources

* A selection of percussion instruments, including some made from metal and some from wood
* Two large signs, one with the heading of 'Metal', the other 'Wood.'

What to do

1. Each child sits in a circle holding a percussion instrument made from metal or wood.
2. You should explain to the children: When I hold up the sign saying 'Metal', anyone who has a metal instrument can play. When I hold up the sign saying 'Wood', anyone who has a wooden instrument can play.
3. Take turns in holding up the 'Metal'/'Wood' signs and both at the same time.
4. Ask the children to listen to each category carefully and write down or describe the sounds made when metal instruments are played as opposed to when wooden instruments are played.

Variations

- Ask a child to take charge of the 'Metal'/'Wood' signs and lead the game.
- The children could be asked to play their instruments in a particular way, such as softly, loudly, quickly or slowly.
- The instruments can be rotated around the group to ensure that the children understand the concept.

Shake, Strike or Blow

Shake, Strike or Blow is a useful game for teaching children about the different ways in which instruments can be played.

Suitable for

KS1

Aims

- To develop an understanding that different instruments require different actions to make them produce sound.
- To build experience in playing a range of percussion instruments.

Resources

- A selection of instruments, including some which need to be shaken, struck or blown in order for them to make a sound
- Three large hula hoops
- Labels – Shake/Strike/Blow

What to do

1. The children form a circle around three large hula hoops. Each hula hoop should have a label of shake, strike or blow.

2. Give an instrument to every child in the circle, explaining: 'When it is your turn, you need to place your instrument carefully in the hoop which you think your instrument belongs to. Do you shake it, strike it or blow it?'

3. Once the instruments are placed in the hoops, start a discussion about any which are in the wrong hoop, and any instruments which could be placed in more than one hoop.

Variations

- Ask the children to devise their own way of categorising the selection of instruments.
- Try asking the children to identify the name of the instrument and play it correctly before placing it in the hoop.
- You could extend the activity by using a selection of woodwind, brass and percussion instruments and labelling the hoops accordingly.

Catch You Out!

Catch You Out is an exciting rhythm game which can be used as a music lesson warm-up or a main activity. The children will have to concentrate and listen very carefully if they do not want to be caught out!

Suitable for

KS1, KS2

Aims

* To listen with concentration and to internalise and recall sounds with increasing aural memory.
* To perform rhythmic phrases with attention to detail.

Resources

* Class set of untuned percussion instruments and one for the leader of the game

What to do

1. The children and teacher form a circle holding an untuned instrument each.
2. Play the children a simple rhythm on your instrument.
3. The children repeat the rhythm on their instruments.
4. Play a different rhythm on your instrument and the children repeat it.
5. Repeat steps 2–4 for as long as you wish, changing the rhythm every time. Then choose to play the same rhythm pattern twice in a row. When the children recognise the repeat, they stop and do not play it back to you. Any child who begins to play the repeated rhythm has been caught out!

Variations

- You could choose an able child to take over the role of the leader and play the rhythms.
- When children are caught out by the leader, they could put their instrument down and remain out of the game until the leader starts a new game. You could give stickers or reward points to the last five children who have not been caught out.
- Why not have the children clap the rhythm back rather than use instruments? This makes the game quicker to play and organise.
- You could sing simple melodic phrases instead of playing rhythmic ones; the children could sing them back to you until you choose to repeat a phrase.

Code Breakers

Code Breakers is a versatile game which works to improve listening and performing skills. Children pass a message/code around the group, listen intently to see if it changes, and respond accordingly.

Suitable for

KS1, KS2

Aims

* To encourage children to listen, watch and wait for their turn when performing.
* To identify and perform small changes in rhythm or melody.

Resources

* Class set of percussion instruments (optional)

What to do

1. The children form a circle. This can be as a whole class initially, then in smaller groups.

2. Explain to the children: 'I am going to play a rhythm code. This rhythm will then pass around the circle from one person to the next. There might be small changes in the rhythm as it travels from one person to the next. This is okay. You need to try and copy the rhythm which is passed to you.' (The children can either clap the rhythm or use percussion instruments.)

3. Once the rhythm has travelled around the group, you can compare the rhythm which was played at the beginning with the one which arrived back at the end, in a similar fashion to the game of Chinese Whispers.

4. A challenge can be set to see if the rhythm can travel around the circle without changing.

Variations

- The children could take turns to be the leader and start the game by playing a rhythm to travel around the circle.
- A melody can be sung by the leader and passed around the circle in place of a rhythm.
- Once the children are confident with the game the rules can be changed so that anyone who changes the rhythm on its way around the circle is out.

Mood Music

Mood music is a fascinating activity which encourages children to listen to music and record their responses. It can be used to bring out children's ideas about the emotions and images created by music. The activity can also focus on particular musical elements such as instruments, timbre, rhythm or pitch.

Suitable for

KS1, KS2

Aims

- To develop listening and appraising skills.
- To explore and express ideas and feelings about music.
- To listen to a range of music from different times and cultures.

Resources

- Selection of CDs or songs from a variety of musical genres/styles (a selection which demonstrates a variety of emotions)
- Recording sheets/paper/individual whiteboards for children to record ideas on

What to do

1. Explain to the children: 'You are going to listen to a piece of music. You might find it easier to concentrate if you close your eyes. I want you to try and create a picture in your mind as you listen to the music; try to decide how the music makes you feel. When the music stops I want you to draw the picture that you saw in your mind and write any words (or draw pictures) which describe how the music made you feel.'

2. Ask the children to share some of their responses with a partner or with the whole class. Reassure the children that it is normal for people to respond in different ways to a piece of music and that there is no correct answer in this activity.

3. A second piece of music can then be listened to following the same procedure. The second piece of music could be one which creates a very different mood or emotion from the first.

This version is the activity in one of its simplest forms. You can ask children to focus on a particular musical element such as: the instruments used and when they appear in the piece of music, the techniques which the composer used to create the mood in the piece, or elements such as pitch, timbre, lyrics, melody and rhythm. You could adapt the way in which the children record their responses according to the focus of the listening task by creating a specific recording sheet (see Tables 5.1 and 5.2).

Variations

- The children can be asked to design and create a CD cover/sleeve artwork which reflects the mood of the piece of music.
- Children can create a storyboard for a video to accompany the piece of music which reflects the themes or emotions in the music. The actual video could then be shown to the children if available. Older children may be able to create/film their own videos.
- The activity can be extended into a composition session in which the children create music based on a particular mood/emotion.
- If the children have a broad knowledge of musical elements and have good listening skills, they can be asked to evaluate a piece of music with a focus on several areas at once (see Table 5.2).

Table 5.1

Name:	Instruments used at beginning:
Music Title: Composer: Mood created:	
Instruments used in middle:	Instruments used at end:

Table 5.2

Name:	Tempo (speed):
Music Title: Composer:	
Instruments used:	Mood:
Dynamics:	Pitch:

These and additional images are available to view/download from the companion website at **www.pearsoned.co.uk/barron**.

Musical Words

Musical Words is a useful activity which can assist children when composing melodies. Words are created using musical note names and then played using tuned instruments. Musical Words can be an activity in its own right, or used as a tool to prompt improvisation when composing in groups.

Suitable for

KS1, KS2

Aims

- To improvise and develop melodic material.
- To play tuned instruments with control and accuracy.
- To make improvements to their own work.

Resources

- Selection of tuned instruments (glockenspiels, xylophones, chime bars, keyboards with note names displayed on keys, etc.)
- Multiple sets of musical note letter cards (C,D,E,F,G,A,B) (optional)
- Paper/whiteboards and pens

What to do

1. Explain the note names C,D,E,F,G,A,B, and write them on a board. Play these notes on a tuned instrument such as a keyboard, and discuss what happens as the list goes on from C to B (the notes get higher in pitch). You should then play the notes in reverse order for the children.

2. Ask the class to think of a word which can be made using the note letters, emphasising that the letters can be repeated.

3. Play the musical note words which the children suggest on the keyboard, e.g. B A G.

4. Explain to the children: 'You are going to work in pairs/groups to make your own musical words and then play them using tuned instruments. Try repeating the words to make a musical phrase such as B A G, B A G, B A G. You can write down your list of musical words and choose your favourites. Try putting two or three different words together, play them and see what happens. See if you can arrange the words in such a way that they make a musical phrase which sounds good.'

5. Allow the children time to create, refine and practise their phrases. Gather the children together to listen to each other's work.

6. After listening, you could lead a discussion on how certain musical words sound better as endings to phrases and others sound better as beginnings.

Variations

- You can simplify the activity by giving the children cards with the note letters on to rearrange into words. Alternatively, the children can be given pre-made musical word cards to play and arrange, i.e.:

BAG

ACE

BAD

DEED

CAGE

AGED

CAGED

BADGE

BAGGAGE

- Why not ask the children to keep their musical words and phrases to be used in later composition sessions where accompaniments can be added with percussion, or lyrics can be added to create songs?
- You could arrange the children's musical words into a longer composition on the board. The class could then perform this piece together and make comments/alterations on the arrangement of the words.

Name that Instrument

Name that Instrument is a fun game which helps children to develop their knowledge of instrument sounds and names.

Suitable for

KS1, KS2

Aims

To develop knowledge of percussion instrument names and the sounds that instruments make.

Resources

- A selection of percussion instruments
- A table and screen to hide the instruments
- Flash cards with pictures of the instruments being used

What to do

1. The children sit facing you, behind the screen (a tabletop whiteboard makes an ideal screen).

2. Explain to the children: 'I am going to play an instrument behind this screen. You will be able to hear the sound it makes, but you will not be able to see it! Your job is to name the instrument that I am playing.'

3. You may choose to show the children the instruments which you have behind the screen and tell them the correct names before you begin the game. Alternatively, you could give out flash cards with instrument pictures, names, or both, for the children to hold up.

Variations

- The number of instruments which you have behind the screen can be decreased to make the game easier, or increased to make the game harder.
- Two instruments could be played at the same time behind the screen to improve the children's ability to recognise multiple/layered sounds.
- You could give control of the game to a child so long as they know the name of the instrument they are playing.

Pass the Beat

Pass the Beat is a game which helps children to gain a sense of pulse or regular beat. It is useful as a whole class warm-up game or as a main activity in smaller groups.

Suitable for

KS1, KS2

Aims

- To play untuned instruments with control and rhythmic accuracy.
- To listen, watch and wait for a turn when performing.

Resources

- Class set of percussion instruments
- CD player and CD (optional)

What to do

1. The children and you form a circle, each holding an untuned percussion instrument.

2. Explain to the children: 'I am going to pass a beat around the circle. You need to play your instrument on the beat as it travels around the circle. I am going to play out four beats before the first person starts, and I will keep playing the beat as it travels around the circle.' The beat will be passed around the circle in the style of a Mexican wave.

3. You may find that children miss their turn/beat to begin with. If this does happen, keep playing the beat until the child plays and then continue around the circle.

Variations

- The children can clap the beat or shout their name or other words/numbers in place of using instruments; this makes the game easier to play and organise.
- Each child can be asked to play four beats on their turn as it passes around the circle. Once playing more than one beat, actions could be incorporated such as knee tap, knee tap, clap, clap, or heads, shoulders, knees and toes.
- Why not choose an able child or a separate group to take over the role of the leader/time keeper? (This should be highlighted as being an important job.)
- When children miss their beat, they have to put their instrument down and remain out of the game until the leader starts a new game.
- You could play a song from a CD with a regular beat during the game. This will show the importance of keeping in time.

Pulse Points

> Pulse Points is a fun and active game which encourages children to move in time and feel the beat in their bodies.

Suitable for

KS1, KS2

Aims

- To recognise a regular beat/pulse.
- To develop an awareness of each beat in a measure/bar.

Resources

- Large clear space (indoors or outdoors)
- Drum/wood block or similar loud percussion instrument
- Metronome (optional)
- CD and CD player (optional)

What to do

1. The children form a circle and listen as you play a repeated phrase on the drum: you need to count, '1, 2, 3, 4,' out loud and play the drum only on beat '1' (the first beat of every bar.) Invite the children to join in by counting '1, 2, 3, 4,' and clapping on the first beat of the bar in time with the drum. A metronome can be introduced and discussed here to make sure that the tempo (speed) remains the same.

2. Once the children are confident with counting and clapping, invite them to move into a space. Explain: 'Instead of clapping on "1", this time you are allowed to take one step, making sure that your foot lands on the floor exactly on "one". You should stand still during beats "2" and "3", and get ready to move when you hear "4". Encourage the children to try to feel the beat in their bodies'.

Once they are confident, you can ask them to stop counting aloud and rely on the beat of the drum and counting in their heads to tell them when to move.

3. Variations can be added, such as a two-footed jump which lands on the first beat of the bar, or movement on every beat of the bar with a bigger movement or jump on '1'.

Variations

- Ask an able child to take the role of leader, allowing you to join in with the children and model the movement/actions.
- A piece of music can be played on a CD player while the children count and move in time. The drum can still be used in this instance to highlight/accent the first beat of the bar.
- The time signature can be changed, e.g. change to 3/4 time by counting: **1**, 2, 3/**1**, 2, 3/**1**, 2, 3.

Silent Tambourine

Silent Tambourine is an excellent way to get a class calm and ready for a music lesson, or any lesson for that matter.

Suitable for

KS1, KS2

Aims

- To settle a class before starting a music lesson.
- To encourage listening and handling instruments with care.

Resources

- Tambourine
- For variations – blindfold/more tambourines/bells

What to do

1. The children form a circle.
2. Give a tambourine to any child in the circle and explain: 'I want the tambourine to travel around the circle making as little noise as possible. If you touch the bells or shake the tambourine it will cause a sound. I really hope you can do it without making a sound!'
3. Collect the tambourine after it has travelled around the circle and ask the children if they could do it more quietly.

Variations

- Extra tambourine/s to be passed around the circle in the opposite direction. Alternative instruments such as bells or rain sticks could be introduced.
- A child can be seated blindfolded in the middle of the circle; they should point to the place where they hear a sound. If they identify the position of the tambourine, they swap places with the child who made the sound.

Sound Pictures

Sound Pictures is a versatile activity which can be used to introduce or reinforce many musical concepts. It uses a basic form of notation and children will quickly learn to follow the conductor.

Suitable for

KS1, KS2

Aims

- To develop confidence in following a musical score.
- To rehearse and perform with others (e.g. starting and finishing together, keeping to a steady pulse).
- To extend their knowledge of musical concepts such as pitch (high/low), dynamics (volume) or tempo (speed).

Resources

- Class set of untuned percussion instruments
- Whiteboard and pens, or alternatives such as large sheets of paper, interactive whiteboard or OHP
- Baton or alternatives such as drum stick or paintbrush

What to do

1. Each child sits facing you, holding a percussion instrument.
2. Draw a line from the bottom left corner of the board/sheet to the top right corner and explain: 'The left side of the board is the start of the piece of music, the right side of the board is the end. When the baton touches the line at the start you begin to play, when it has gone along the line and got to the end, it will be taken off the line and you should stop playing.'

3. Once the children understand the basic principle of a Sound Picture, you can introduce a musical concept such as dynamics (volume). You could explain: 'This time the start of the piece of music will be played quietly. As the baton travels up the line the piece will get louder until the end.'

4. Once the children have mastered this simple diagonal line arrangement, you can draw a more complex line such as a V or W shape, where the volume will increase or decrease a number of times as the piece progresses.

Variations

• The children can use body percussion or voices to perform Sound Pictures.
• You could choose a child to take over the role of the leader and conduct the class using the baton.
• Try inviting a child to create a new Sound Picture by drawing a line on the board/sheet which begins on the left and ends on the right, with an interesting pattern.
• The activity can be extended by asking children to create, rehearse and perform their own Sound Pictures in small groups.

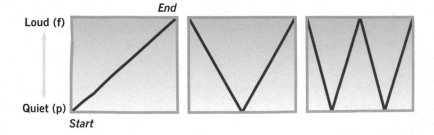

Sound Walk

> Sound Walk is a great activity which encourages the development of listening skills and stimulates children's creativity when recreating sounds.

Suitable for

KS1, KS2

Aims

- To develop listening and recording skills.
- To encourage improvisation with sounds and exploration of timbre (tone colour/quality).
- To respond to non-musical starting points.

Resources

- Paper, pencils and clipboards
- Class set of instruments
- Portable tape recorder/dictaphone/laptop and microphone (optional)

What to do

1. Lead the children on a walk around a predetermined route. This could be inside school, outside in the school grounds, in the local area (provided adequate supervision is available) or a combination of these areas.

2. Choose appropriate places for the children to stop and listen for a minute in silence. The children record on their paper any sounds they can hear at each location. The paper can be divided up into sections and numbered/labelled as to the location of each stop on the Sound Walk. The children can note down the sounds heard

using a combination of written descriptions and pictures. You could also record the sounds using a portable tape player/dictaphone or laptop.

3. The children return to the classroom and work in groups to recreate the stages of the Sound Walk using instruments, voices and body percussion. This can be organised by asking individual groups to recreate one part of the Sound Walk and then they can perform their compositions in turn to replicate the stages of the Walk. Alternatively, all groups can be asked to recreate the whole Sound Walk.

4. The class performance of the Sound Walk can be recorded, then listened to by the children and compared with the sound recordings taken on the Walk.

Story Music

Story Music is an exciting activity which classes of all ages will enjoy. It encourages children to choose appropriate instruments and sounds to accompany the reading of a story. This activity is similar to 'Soundtrack' (see page 177); Story Music may be more suitable for younger children.

Suitable for

KS1, KS2

Aims

- To extend understanding of instruments and the sounds they produce.
- To rehearse and perform with others.
- To explore, choose and organise sounds and musical ideas.

Resources

- Story book with good opportunities for making a musical accompaniment. A big book would be ideal for younger children. (*Little Red Riding Hood* or *The Three Little Pigs* are great choices.)
- Class set of instruments

What to do

1. The children form a circle with an instrument placed on the floor in front of them.

2. Explain to the children: 'We are going to be making music and sound effects to go with a story. I am going to read the story to you now. As I read it, you need to be thinking of ideas for music or sounds which would fit in with the events or mood of the story. I will ask you for your ideas once I have finished reading.'

3. You may wish to give some examples of sound effects/musical moods before the story is read, e.g. knocking, a door opening/closing, wind whistling, scary or fast music.

4. The children listen to the story and share their ideas with the class. You could add post-it notes to the book to indicate: where sound effects need to be played, where there will be a need for background music while the story is read, and places where the story will stop and mood music will be played.

5. Ask each child, one by one, to pick up their instrument, play it, and suggest which sound effects or music in the story it could be used for.

6. Read the story again, while the children play along in the appropriate places. It may take several attempts before the performance is perfected.

Variations

- Simplify the activity by pre-marking points in the story at which obvious sounds would take place, i.e. the closing of a door, the ringing of a bell.
- The children can work in groups to develop Story Music for their own group stories and then share their work with the class.
- Extend the activity by spending time creating longer compositions which are played in pauses in the story to set the scene or describe the mood.
- Encourage the children to use their voices or classroom objects to create sound effects in addition to the use of instruments.
- The final performance of the story can be tape recorded and played back to the children; they can evaluate by highlighting good points and suggesting areas for improvement.

Soundtrack

> Soundtrack is a fantastic activity which children of all ages will enjoy. It encourages them to choose appropriate instruments and sounds to accompany a piece of film.

Suitable for

KS1, KS2

Aims

- To develop understanding of instruments and the sounds they produce.
- To practise, rehearse and present performances with an awareness of the audience.
- To explore, choose and organise sounds and musical ideas.

Resources

- Interactive whiteboard/TV with video or DVD player
- Short clip of film, cartoon, advert, TV programme
- Paper (possibly divided into storyboard-style sections related to the content of the chosen film clip)
- Pencils
- Class set of instruments
- Tape recorder (optional)

What to do

1. Show the children a short film clip on a whiteboard/TV, with the sound turned off. You can lead a discussion about what sounds might be on the soundtrack, i.e. music, sound effects and voices. Show the clip again and ask the children to note down ideas for specific sounds and the point at which they could appear in the clip. The children's soundtrack ideas can be recorded on

storyboard sheets, or they can draw/write the point at which their chosen sound should occur. This process may require the clip to be shown several times.

2. The children can then work in groups to share their ideas for the soundtrack and explore the ways in which they can make their version using instruments, voices and body percussion.

3. Allow the children time to organise and practise their soundtrack performance. You may need to insist that the groups spend a few minutes every so often discussing their work and not playing instruments.

4. The groups can then perform their soundtrack in turn while the film clip is playing. Each time a performance is heard, the non-playing groups can be asked to think of evaluative comments.

5. Once all of the performances have taken place, the actual soundtrack can be turned on and the film clip can be watched and discussed.

Variations

- The activity can be simplified for younger children by creating a more prescriptive storyboard with set points at which more obvious sounds would take place, i.e. the closing of a door, the ringing of a bell. Similarly, older children may not need the film clip to be represented on a storyboard at all, but can develop their own.
- To extend the activity, a longer piece of film can be chosen. This can lead to the children creating longer compositions of appropriately themed music to accompany the clip. There are many IT software packages available which children could use to create a piece of music to accompany the clip. This could act as a backing track while they perform the sound effects by hand using instruments/objects.
- You could divide the film clip into sections. Each group will create and perform one section of the soundtrack.
- Try tape recording the group performances and playing them back with the film clip to allow the pupils to listen to their work.

Ways to Play

Ways to Play is a practical idea which can help children when learning about instruments and rhythms. The children will use ideas cards to help them develop rhythmic phrases. Ways to Play can be an activity in its own right, or used as a tool to prompt improvisation when composing in groups.

Suitable for

KS1, KS2

Aims

- To improvise and develop rhythmic material.
- To play instruments with control and accuracy.
- To make improvements to pupils' own work.

Resources

- Selection of percussion instruments, tuned and untuned
- Multiple sets of Ways to Play cards
- Paper/whiteboards and pens

What to do

1. Turn over the Ways to Play cards to hide their content, then ask a child to pick a card. Then ask a different child to pick an instrument.

2. Demonstrate by playing the chosen instrument in the style suggested on the chosen Ways to Play card, e.g. 2 short sounds, 2 long sounds.

3. Explain to the children: 'You are going to work in pairs/groups, choosing Ways to Play cards and then playing them using instruments. Try repeating the cards to make a rhythmic phrase

such as 2 short sounds, 2 long sounds/2 short sounds, 2 long sounds/2 short sounds, 2 long sounds. Try putting 2 or 3 different cards together and see what happens. Try to arrange the cards in such a way that they make a musical phrase which sounds good.'

4. Allow the children time to create and practise their rhythmic phrases, then gather the class together to listen to each other's work.

5. After listening, you can lead a discussion on how certain cards sound better as endings to phrases and others sound better as beginnings.

Variations

- Try extending the activity by giving children Ways to Play cards which contain the standard notation symbols (music notes) in addition to the descriptions of the sounds. Eventually, the sound descriptions can be removed, leaving only the standard notation on the cards for the children to play.
- The children can create their own Ways to Play cards, using descriptions/note values, or both.
- You could sort the Ways to Play cards into a longer composition on the board. The class can then perform this piece together and make comments/alterations on the arrangement of the phrases.
- You can ask the children to keep their card arrangements to be used in later composition sessions where further layers of rhythm or melodies can be added.

Ways to Play Cards Example

1 short sound	2 short sounds	3 short sounds	1 short sound	2 short sounds	3 short sounds
2 quiet sounds	4 quiet sounds	1 loud sound	3 loud sounds	1 long and 2 short sounds	2 short and 1 long sound
2 low sounds	4 high sounds	1 low sound and 1 high sound	4 low sounds and 4 high sounds	1 shake sound and 1 tap sound	3 shake sounds and 1 crash sound

eighth note ♪	quarter note ♩	half note ♩	whole note o
eighth note ♪	quarter note ♩	half note ♩	whole note o

These and additional images are available to view/download from the companion website at **www.pearsoned.co.uk/barron**.

Beat It!

Beat It! is a great opportunity for children to play as part of a class/group orchestra with a clear structure. It teaches them to follow a basic musical score.

Suitable for

KS2

Aims

- To play tuned and untuned instruments with control and rhythmic accuracy.
- To rehearse and perform with others, e.g. starting and finishing together, keeping to a steady pulse.
- To improve the ability to follow a musical score.

Resources

- Class set of percussion instruments
- Beat It! grid on paper, drawn on whiteboard, or created on interactive whiteboard

What to do

1. The children sit facing the Beat It! grid, holding a percussion instrument. Make sure that they know which category their instrument comes from — skin, wood or metal. You could ask the pupils to hold up their instrument when you say the category name, i.e. 'wood'.

2. Explain: 'When your number is in a shaded square you play one beat on that number, in the other squares you rest, which means you don't play.'

3. Take the role of timekeeper, saying and clapping, '1,2,3,4', repeatedly. Ask the skin group alone to practise their part with you first, i.e. playing a beat on 1 and 3 while you count, '1,2,3,4'. Similarly, ask the wood and metal groups to practise alone with you.

4. Once the children are confident with their parts, then the Beat It! grid can be played by all, making sure that the children are following you/the timekeeper who can point to each number as each bar progresses if necessary.

Beat It! Grid Example

Skin	1	2	3	4
Wood	1	2	3	4
Metal	1	2	3	4

Variations

- The grid can be reduced to one or two parts. The parts can be made easier to play by just having one beat to play, or by playing on every beat.
- Children can clap the rhythm back in place of using instruments, thus making the game quicker to play and organise.
- When the class is confident the teacher can stop counting out loud or pointing to the numbers.
- The Beat It! grid can be changed by shading different squares. The grid can be extended to two or more bars of music, and still be repeated.
- Why not ask the children to create and perform their own Beat It! grids in groups?
- The children could discuss and make notes on important things to remember when playing music with others in a group or orchestra.

Syllable Patterns

Syllable Patterns, or 'Tea/Coffee', is a great way of introducing children to rhythmic phrases. Words are used as an introduction to learning standard notation values (music notes).

Suitable for

KS2

Aims

- To develop and improvise rhythmic material when performing.
- To develop experience of performing accurately with others.
- To extend knowledge of note values.

Resources

- Whiteboard
- Class set of untuned percussion instruments (optional)

What to do

1. The children form a circle. You need to clap four notes out slowly and count out each beat as, '1, 2, 3, 4'. Then repeat the clapping but replace the counting of '1,2,3,4' with the words 'Tea, tea, tea, tea' (or any other short one-syllable word).

2. Invite the children to join in with you by clapping and saying 'Tea, tea, tea, tea'. They may need reminding to keep a steady speed/tempo with their clapping.

3. When the children are used to this, try clapping eight beats, twice as fast as before and count each beat as, '1, 2, 3, 4, 5, 6, 7, 8'. You can then repeat the clapping, but replace the pairs of beats

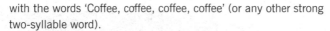

with the words 'Coffee, coffee, coffee, coffee' (or any other strong two-syllable word).

4. Invite the children to join in again by saying 'Coffee, coffee, coffee, coffee'. They may need reminding to keep a steady speed/tempo with their clapping.

5. Once the class is confident with both of these aspects, you can split it into two groups and have both the tea and coffee patterns playing at the same time. The groups can then swap parts and try again

Variations

- Give the children percussion instruments with which to play their part.
- The class could create phrases using the words 'tea' and 'coffee' to create a longer rhythmic pattern to be played by clapping or with percussion instruments, e.g. 'Tea, tea, coffee, coffee, tea'. This can be done in groups; the children can rehearse and perform their variations to each other.
- Teach the children the names of these note lengths in standard notation, i.e. crotchet (tea), quaver/quaver (coffee), and the standard symbols:

crotchet or quarter note: ♩

quaver/s or eighth note/s: ♪ ♫

Pupils can then use these notes to create their own rhythmic patterns.
- You could try playing out a rhythmic phrase using a mixture of crotchets and quavers; the children can attempt to repeat it using claps or instruments. Follow this by asking them to write down the rhythm using music notes.

Chapter 6
PE

PE

In this section you will find activities mainly focused upon the gymnastic, athletic and games elements of Physical Education.

Most of the activities are adaptable to use as a warm-up/cool-down, or extendable to use as a main lesson activity.

Some of the activities make use of standard school PE equipment such as bean bags or bands, while others can be done without resources. Many of the activities encourage the children to be involved in developing a game; this will increase their enjoyment and bring a sense of ownership.

PE tips

- Always remind children about the health and safety implications of any activity before beginning it.
- Activities/games can be adapted by changing the size of the playing area, the number of players, the time limit/speed or the amount/type of equipment.
- Encourage children to set their own targets.
- Encourage peer support and evaluation when developing skills.

Band Race

Band Race is a competitive warm-up game in which two or more teams compete to collect the most bands.

Suitable for

KS1, KS2

Aims

- To raise the heart rate and prepare the body for exercise.
- To take part in and design challenges and competitions that call for speed and power.

Resources

- Whistle
- Bands or small objects which can be carried easily and safely
- Coloured marker/cone

What to do

1. Divide the class into groups of equal numbers. Ask the children to form lines, standing two paces apart, all facing forwards, while standing behind a start line.

2. Explain to the children: 'When the whistle blows, the children at the front of each line run to the marker, the first child to reach the marker will pick up a band and return it to their team, the others will return empty-handed. The winning team is the one with the highest number of bands at the end of the game. If two children reach the marker at exactly the same time then both will be given a band. While you are waiting for your turn you can jog on the spot'.

3. You may need to tell the children that they are not allowed to try to stop or impede each other when trying to collect a band. You should stand near the marker to put out a new band each time.

Variations

- Why not vary the way in which the children travel to collect the band, e.g. jumping, side-stepping or skipping?
- Small cones/markers can be used to set out a course for the children to weave around before collecting a band.
- You could invite the children to design their own version of this game.

Cat and Mouse

Cat and Mouse is a traditional tag game. The mice need to travel and turn quickly if they are going to avoid being caught by the cats!

Suitable for

KS1, KS2

Aims

- To raise the heart rate and prepare the body for exercise.
- To take part in and design challenges and competitions that call for speed and precision.
- To encourage awareness of others and quick reactions.

Resources

- Class set of bands or tag rugby tags

What to do

1. Give a band to everyone in the class apart from two children who will become the cats. Ask the children to stand in a space.

2. Explain to the children: 'If you have a band, that means you are a mouse and you need to tuck the end of the band into the back of your shorts to make a mouse tail! If you don't have a band, that means you are a cat. The cats will be trying to catch the mice by taking their tails! The mice can move in any direction, but once a cat has removed your tail, you are out. The winning cat will be the one with the most tails at the end of the game.'

3. You may wish to remind the children to be careful not to make contact with anybody else when moving around.

Variations

- Children who are out can do skipping exercises to keep warm until the next game begins.
- You could set a time limit for the cats to catch mice. After the time is up, any mice that remain can become the cats in the next game.
- The number of cats can be increased to make the game easier.
- The mice that have been caught can become cats straight away to make the game faster.
- One or more of the mice can be given a bean bag at the beginning of the game. If a cat catches a mouse with a bean bag, this is worth five extra points.

Colours

Colours is a simple warm-up game which encourages quick thinking and movement. It can be successfully linked with a Modern Foreign Language (MFL).

Suitable for

KS1, KS2

Aims

- To raise the heart rate and prepare the body for exercise.
- To take part in challenges that call for precision, speed and power.

Resources

- Assortment of different coloured PE equipment: bean bags, hula hoops, markers, quoits, etc.
- Skipping ropes
- Whistle (optional)

What to do

1. Put out a selection of different coloured equipment all around the playing area.

2. Explain to the children: 'I am going to call out a colour. You then need to go and touch an object of that colour. The last one to do this will be out. When you are out, you need to stand in the "out area" and do some skipping.'

3. You may wish to mention that there is to be no physical contact, and anybody who impedes another child will be out.

4. The game continues until a winner, or winning group, remains.

Variations

- You can increase or decrease the number of coloured objects to make the game easier or harder.
- An alternative game is to make the children run to hold any colour when the whistle blows. The teacher then chooses one colour to be out. Any children who are holding this colour are out of the game. This can be an effective game when played with younger children as they can be asked to stand inside a choice of coloured hula hoops, before discovering which colour is out.
- You can call out the colour in a foreign language (MFL).

Follow the Drum

Follow the Drum is a great game in which children perform different actions depending on how many drumbeats they hear.

Suitable for

KS1, KS2

Aims

- To raise the heart rate and prepare the body for exercise.
- To take part in and design challenges and competitions that call for stamina and precision.
- To use running and jumping skills in combination.

Resources

- Drum (or any other loud percussion instrument) and beater

What to do

1. Advise the children not to make physical contact with anyone in this game and encourage them to use all of the available space safely.

2. Explain to the children: 'You are going to be travelling around the space in any direction. When you hear the drum play one beat you need to do one jump into the air, and then carry on travelling. When you hear the drum play two beats you need to crouch down and touch the ground with both hands, and then carry on travelling. When you hear the drum play three beats you need to clap your hands in front of you, then behind you, and then you carry on travelling'. (You can alter these actions to suit the age and ability of the children.)

4. You can add more instructions for four and five drumbeats once the children are used to the game.

Variations

- Why not ask the children to travel in a certain way in between the drumbeat actions, such as hopping, jumping or skipping?
- You could ask a child to take over the role of playing the drumbeats.
- You could invite the children to design their own version of this game.
- You can decrease the length of the intervals in between each drum action, thus making the children switch between exercises more quickly. This can build up into a big finish where you play the drumbeats in a very quick sequence to see if any of the children can keep up!

Keep it Up

Keep it Up is a useful and adaptable game which encourages quick thinking, movement and teamwork. The children will enjoy competing in teams to achieve the best score.

Suitable for

KS1, KS2

Aims

- To raise the heart rate and prepare the body for exercise.
- To take part in challenges and competitions that call for speed, agility and accuracy.
- To develop striking and fielding skills.

Resources

- Balloons (five per group, plus a few spares)
- Balls/shuttles/bean bags/racquets (optional)
- Dome markers

What to do

1. Divide the class into equal teams and mark out a suitable playing area for each team.

2. Explain to the children: 'When I say go, the first person will enter the area and try to keep one balloon afloat by tapping it up into the air. After ten seconds without the balloon falling, a second balloon should be passed in by a team member; if the player manages to keep both balloons afloat for ten seconds then a third and fourth can be added. The player must stay inside the area'.

3. The children take turns at being the player keeping the balloons afloat.

Variations

- The size of the playing area can be increased/decreased to make the game easier or harder.
- The game can be turned into a competition by stating that the first team to keep up three balloons wins, but if a balloon falls before this happens, then the player must be replaced with the next team member.
- Try using balls, shuttles or bean bags in the same way. You could allow more than one player in the playing area.
- Why not make the balloon game more difficult by using only one balloon, which must be kept afloat with a forehand tap, then a backhand tap, followed by a knee tap? Once the player completes 20 touches, the next player takes over without the balloon touching the ground.

Musical Moves

Musical Moves is a selection of aerobic style warm-up activities. They can be used to introduce/practise skills needed for the main lesson focus.

Suitable for

KS1, KS2

Aims

- To raise the heart rate and prepare the body for exercise.
- To take part in challenges that call for speed, stamina and power
- To develop specific skills for main lesson objectives.

Resources

- CD player and CDs
- Selection of appropriate PE equipment; this can be chosen in relation to the main lesson activity

What to do

1. Circuit Training. Divide the class into five groups which will rotate around five different activity stations which should be labelled accordingly. The children keep doing their activity until the music stops, and then they move on to the next challenge. Activities for circuit training stages could be: star jumps, jogging on the spot, skipping, step-ups on to a bench or squat thrusts. Alternatively the activities could focus on a particular skill in preparation for the main lesson activity such as: bouncing a basketball, throwing and catching a ball/bean bag or dribbling a football between two markers.

2. **Aerobic Workout.** Lead a workout of movements in time to a piece of music. The children copy the movements in a space. The workout should become progressively more intense to raise the heart rate. The children can take turns to lead the class workout once they have learned a range of appropriate movements. Children can create a plan for their turn at leading the aerobic exercises which charts the actions and the order in which they want the other children to perform them.

3. **Musical Moves.** Call out an action or method of travelling and then play the music. The children perform the action or movement until the music stops. They must then sit down and do some leg-stretching exercises until the next action is called out.

Numbers

Numbers is a simple warm-up game which encourages quick thinking, movement and teamwork. It can be successfully linked with a Modern Foreign Language (MFL).

Suitable for

KS1, KS2

Aims

- To raise the heart rate and prepare the body for exercise.
- To take part in and design challenges and competitions that call for speed and power.
- To work with others to keep games going.

Resources

- CD player and CD (optional)

What to do

1. Invite the children to stand in a space. Explain to the children: 'When the music starts, you need to travel around the room by side-stepping (you can choose any exercise or movement to be done here). When the music stops, I am going to call out a number. You need to quickly get into groups of that number and sit down together. When the music starts you leave your group and go back to side-stepping in a space'.

2. After several turns at calling out different numbers, you may wish to change the movement which is to be done in between the grouping tasks.

3. You may need to introduce a rule that no group is allowed to refuse a child into their group before they sit down.

Variations

- Try including a rule that any group which sits down with the wrong number of members is called out. They leave the game until a new round begins.
- Similarly, the last children to sit down in a group of the required number can be called out. They leave the game until a new round begins.
- Why not call out the numbers in a foreign language?
- The game can be played without the use of music. In this case it may be useful to blow a whistle before announcing the number.

Pirates

Pirates is a traditional game which children love. They become pirates and perform a collection of movements when the action is called.

Suitable for

KS1, KS2

Aims

- To raise the heart rate and prepare the body for exercise.
- To take part in and design challenges and competitions that call for speed and power.
- To remember and repeat actions accurately.

Resources

- None

What to do

1. The children sit in the centre of the hall in two rows which meet at the beginning and end, making the outline of a pirate ship. They should perform a rowing action.
2. Call out one of the commands from the list on page 204, which the children perform. The teacher calls out a different command and the children change their actions accordingly.

Pirate Command	Action Required
Walk the Plank	Walk with one foot in front of the other with arms outstretched for ten steps and then jump.
Pirate Ship	Return to the centre of the hall. Make the ship outline and row.
Climb the Rigging	Climb an imaginary rope ladder.
Fire the Cannons	Get into pairs, light the fuse and jump up, shouting 'Boom!'
Storm Ahead	Move sideways and up and down as if riding huge waves.
Scrub the Decks	Get down on hands and knees and pretend to scrub the floor.
Man Overboard	Jump and then swim back to the pirate ship.

Variation

- Why not invite the children to think of their own pirate game commands? These can be included in the class repertoire.

Remote Control

Remote Control is an exciting warm-up game which children will enjoy. The teacher holds a remote control which the children must obey!

Suitable for

KS1, KS2

Aims

* To raise the heart rate and prepare the body for exercise.
* To take part in and design challenges and competitions that call for speed, precision and power.
* To remember and repeat actions accurately.

Resources

* Remote control

What to do

1. Invite the children to stand in a space.
2. Explain to the children: 'I have a magic remote control which controls people! When I press and say the function, it will make you do as it says! If I press play, you will travel in any direction. If I press fast forward, you will move quickly in any direction. If I press rewind, you will move backwards carefully. If I press eject, you will crouch down and then jump up. If I press slow motion, you will move around very slowly. If I change the channel, you will change direction. If I press pause, you will freeze until I press another button.'

3. Begin by using two simple commands and then gradually introduce the others. You may wish to remind the class to be aware of other children moving near them, and to be extremely careful if moving backwards.

Variations

- Control of the remote can be given to a child.
- You could use cards with the commands and their symbols on to show the children which action to do, rather than saying the commands.
- The action for the command 'play' can be changed to actions such as skipping with ropes or star jumps.
- Why not develop actions for certain television programmes? These can be used when changing the channel on the remote control. For example, when you give a 'change channel' command you could say the programme which is on. Here are some suggestions: motor racing (moving around quickly and steering), *Bob the Builder* (shovelling or laying bricks), tennis (serving or hitting the ball).

Snakes

Snakes is an enjoyable warm-up game in which children take turns to be the head, body or tail.

Suitable for

KS1, KS2

Aims

- To raise the heart rate and prepare the body for exercise.
- To take part in challenges and competitions that call for speed and power.

Resources

- Whistle
- Balls/bean bags (optional)

What to do

1. The children form groups of five and make lines standing five paces apart, all facing in the same direction/forwards.

2. Explain to the children: 'You are going to be a snake which follows the leader (the head). When the whistle blows once, the person at the back of the line (the tail) moves up to the front and becomes the head. You can move in any direction, but do not get too close to the person in front of you, and be careful if any other snakes cross your path. When you hear the whistle blow twice, everyone stops and your snake needs to return to me'.

3. You can choose the speed at which the snakes move. Begin by walking slowly and gradually get faster until the children are jogging.

Variations

- If the playing surface has courts marked out, then the snakes can try to follow the lines and avoid the other snakes.
- The head of the snake can carry a ball which is passed on when the new head moves forward. If the ball is dropped, then the snake is out.
- You could vary the way in which the snakes travel, i.e. side-stepping, skipping or jumping.
- Small cones could be set out for the snakes to weave between.
- You can set up games for the snakes to play in a stationary position, such as passing balls or bean bags back along their length.

The Bean Game

The Bean Game is a traditional and useful activity for warm-ups in PE. It requires no resources to play and can be extended as the children learn more commands.

Suitable for

KS1, KS2

Aims

- To raise the heart rate and prepare the body for exercise.
- To take part in and design challenges and competitions that call for speed, accuracy and power.
- To remember and repeat actions accurately.

Resources

- None

What to do

1. Ask the children to stand in a space. Explain some of the bean commands from the list on page 210.
2. You should call out one of the commands from the list, which the class will perform in a space. You should then call out a different command and the children change their actions accordingly.

Bean Command	Action Required
Runner Bean	Run on the spot.
Broad Bean	Stretch out arms and legs as wide as possible.
Beanstalk	Crouch down then slowly reach up to the sky.
Jelly Bean	Wobble or shake up and down.
Baked Bean	Lie down as if sunbathing.
Jumping Bean	Jump up and down.
Frozen Bean	Stand still in a frozen pose.

Variations

- Why not invite the children to think of their own bean game commands? These can be included in the class repertoire.
- The children can perform most of the actions by staying in the same space. You might want to adapt some or all of the actions so that they move around while performing them.

Traffic Lights

> Traffic Lights is a fun warm-up game which encourages children to watch for signals and remember the correct actions.

Suitable for

KS1, KS2

Aims

- To raise the heart rate and prepare the body for exercise.
- To take part in and design challenges and competitions that call for speed, accuracy and power.
- To remember and repeat actions accurately.

Resources

- Three coloured items (red/amber/green). These items could be large card circles, cones or bands.

What to do

1. Ask the children to stand in a space.
2. Explain to the children: 'You are going to be cars and follow the instructions given by the traffic lights. When I hold up the red item, that means stop and stand still. When I hold up the amber item, that means do star jumps in a space (or any exercise I choose). When I hold up the green item, that means go and jog around, making sure that you do not make contact with anybody else (or travel in any way which you or the children could choose). You will need to know which coloured item is being held up, and be aware of the people around you at all times.'

Variations

- The instructions for each colour can be adapted by you to fit in with the PE lesson objectives. For example: in a football lesson the amber item could signal jumping and heading an imaginary ball.
- You could pick out the last child to notice the traffic lights changing, who is then out of the game and must stand on the sidelines doing star jumps or skipping.
- You can increase the activity level/pace of the activities as the children get warmed up.
- Why not ask a child to take control of the traffic light objects?

Chapter 7
PSHE

PSHE

In the PSHE section you will find lots of versatile circle time activities which have strong links with speech and language development, as well as with encouraging the self-esteem and emotional awareness of your children.

It is advisable to develop a set of circle time rules before beginning any of the activities. Ideally the rules should be made and agreed with the children.

A ball has been used as an example of a talking object in the activity explanations in this section, but there are many alternatives, such as a teddy or a microphone.

Suggested circle time rules

- Listen to each other.
- Respect other people's ideas.
- Wait your turn and don't interrupt.
- Speak when you have the ball or talking object.
- Pass the ball or talking object if you want to.

Detective

Detective is a versatile circle time game where children have to ask appropriate questions and act on the answers in order to discover the chosen object.

Suitable for

KS1, KS2

Aims

- To encourage the asking of appropriate/relevant closed questions.
- To listen to other people, and play and work cooperatively.
- To develop subject-specific knowledge and understanding.

Resources

- Selections of objects, i.e. pencil cases, coats, books, lunchboxes, instruments or shoes. The objects could be of one type, i.e. only lunchboxes; alternatively, a mixture of items can be used

What to do

1. The children should ideally sit in a circle. Remind the class of the circle time rules (see PSHE introduction page for suggestions).

2. Lay out a group of objects in the centre of the circle.

3. Explain to the children: 'I am going to choose one object from the group in the centre of the circle. It is your job to be detectives and discover which object I am thinking of. You are allowed to ask one question each and I can only answer "yes" or "no." It is your turn to ask a question when the ball is passed to you. Make sure that you listen carefully to all of the questions and answers. Once you are confident that you know which object I am thinking about, then you are allowed to guess when you get the ball'.

4. Once the detectives have discovered the object, you can choose a different object or change the objects, and the game begins again.

Variations

- The children could remove objects from the group which have been eliminated after a question has been answered. This can continue until one object remains in the centre of the circle.
- The ball can be passed around the circle from one child to the next, or passed to children who have their hands up and want to ask a question.
- The objects in the centre of the circle can be specifically chosen to introduce/reinforce a subject learning objective. For example, the objects could be a selection of different rock types (Science), objects made from different materials (DT/Science), musical instruments (Music), or shapes (Numeracy).
- A limit can be set on the number of questions which can be asked by the children. This will encourage them to ask good questions and not repeat any which have already been asked.
- The game can be played without any objects at all. You could write an object name on a whiteboard and conceal your choice. The children then have to guess what the teacher has written down.
- A child can take on the role of the leader by choosing an object and answering the questions. It may be advisable to have them share their answer with the teacher to begin with, meaning that the child in charge can ask for advice if any tricky questions arise.

Emotions

Emotions is an interesting and thought-provoking activity which allows children to express their thoughts, feelings and worries in the safety of the circle time environment.

Suitable for

KS1, KS2

Aims

- To talk about issues, opinions and views.
- To explore personal thoughts and feelings.
- To build personal confidence when speaking in circle time.

Resources

- Circle time ball/object to signify whose turn it is

What to do

1. Have the children form a circle. Remind the class of the circle time rules, emphasising the fact that children can pass at any point and not answer if they do not wish to (see PSHE introduction page for suggestions).

2. Explain to the children: 'We are going to be talking about our feelings and emotions. We all know that sometimes we feel happy or sad. Can you think of something which makes you happy? Are you happy to share it with the rest of the class?'

3. You can then decide whether to pass the ball around the circle, or ask children to put their hands up to ask for a turn.

4. The same routine can be used to discuss things which make us sad, angry, worried, etc. Quite often these sessions will lead on to deeper and meaningful discussions.

Variations

- If children find it difficult to give responses, then a timeframe can be set such as, 'Think of something which has made you happy today', etc.
- Once children are experienced with the circle time format and able to give appropriate responses, the opportunity may arise for them to suggest answers/responses to other children's worries or things which make them sad or angry. This can be a useful opportunity to address issues such as anger management or bereavement.

I Think You're Great!

I Think You're Great! is a circle time game which builds self-esteem by encouraging children to give and receive compliments. It provides an opportunity for children to feel valued for their positive actions and relationships.

Suitable for

KS1, KS2

Aims

* To recognise their worth as individuals by identifying positive things about themselves.
* To provide an opportunity for praising positive actions and good behaviour.

Resources

* Circle time ball/object to signify whose turn it is

What to do

1. Invite the children to sit in a circle. Remind the class of the circle time rules (see PSHE introduction page for suggestions).

2. Explain to the children: 'I am going to roll the ball to someone in the circle; I will then say "I think you're great because . . . ," and then I will give a reason why. The reason I give could be: something I like about that person, something they have done which impressed me, something kind which they did for me, or something which I know they are good at.'

3. Roll the ball to a child and say: 'I think you're great because . . .' (giving a reason why). That child then rolls the ball to another child and repeats the phrase: 'I think you're great because . . .'

4. The game can continue while you encourage children to make sure that everyone is being included. You may wish to ask children to roll the ball to those who have not yet been chosen.

5. The game concludes when everyone has paid and received a compliment. A discussion can then take place to describe how it felt to give and receive a compliment.

Variations

- Children can be asked to give compliments based on one particular aspect such as good behaviour, academic achievements or hobbies/skills to coincide with the theme of a longer PSHE session.
- If the children are finding it difficult to devise compliments then a list of suggestions can be written on a whiteboard for them to choose from.

Language Challenge (MFL)

> Language Challenge is a series of activities designed to introduce or reinforce children's learning of key words and phrases from a Modern Foreign Language (MFL).

Suitable for

KS1, KS2

Aims

- To develop knowledge of how to use and respond to a modern foreign language.
- To develop the ability to discriminate sounds, identify meaning and develop auditory awareness.

Resources

- Circle time ball/object to signify whose turn it is (× 2)
- Hat containing MFL vocabulary cards with English translations
- CD player and CD of music from chosen MFL country

What to do

1. Have the children sit in a circle.

2. The following games can be played in any order; they can be easily differentiated to suit the ability of your class. The games are a very useful way of starting an MFL lesson.

   A. *Numbers*. Write the numbers 1 to 5 in English and in a chosen MFL on the whiteboard; the range for the numbers written will depend on the children's prior knowledge and ability. The children rehearse counting from 1 to 5 together several times. You should then explain: 'I am going to pass the ball around the circle. The first person to receive it will say "1" in [MFL], the second person will say "2" in [MFL]; once we reach 5, the next person will start again at 1.'

B. *Colours 1.* Write a list of colours in English and in a chosen MFL. The children practise reading from the list together. Then explain: 'I am going to pass the ball around the circle. When you receive it you need to say your favourite colour loudly and clearly in [MFL].'

C. *Colours 2.* Hand out pieces of different coloured card to every child in the circle. Explain to the children: 'I am going to choose a colour and say it in [MFL]. If you are holding a card made from that colour, you must stand. Once all of the correct children are standing I will choose a different colour.'

D. *The Hat Game.* Explain to the children: 'I am going to play a piece of music from [Spain/France]. The hat [sombrero/beret] will be passed around the group. When the music stops, the person with the hat will pick a card from it and read aloud what it says in [MFL]. The other children will put up their hands if they know what the word or phrase means, and the person with the card will choose someone to say their answer. This continues until the correct answer is given. Then the music starts again, and the hat moves on around the circle.'

E. *Greetings.* Explain to the children: 'I am going to pass two balls in opposite directions around the circle. When the music stops the person with ball 1 gets to choose a greeting from the list on the whiteboard and say it; the person with ball 2 chooses an appropriate reply and says it. The music will start again and the game continues'.

Ideas for simplification/extension

- Colours 1 can be adapted for use with many types of MFL vocabulary such as food and hobbies.
- Colours 2 can be adapted so that, when you call out a colour in MFL, all the children have to go and touch something in the classroom which is that colour.
- Once the children have developed a good range of basic vocabulary, then games such as Colours and Greetings can be played without the aid of MFL words being displayed.

Liar, Liar!

Liar, Liar! is an entertaining game in which children perform actions in the centre of the circle. Children will need to convey actions and ideas without the aid of speech.

Suitable for

KS1, KS2

Aims

- To use dramatic techniques to convey actions and ideas.
- To develop relationships through play.
- To begin to understand the importance of telling the truth

Resources

- Action cards (optional)

What to do

1. Ask the class to sit in a circle.
2. Explain to the children: 'I am going to choose someone to go to the centre of the circle and act something out without talking; they could pretend to climb a tree, for example. They will point to someone sitting in the circle, who needs to immediately ask them: "What are you doing?" The person in the middle tells a lie about the action they are performing such as: "I'm walking the dog." The person who asked the question then has to go to the centre of the circle and act out the lie, i.e. walking the dog. They then choose someone else to ask them the question'.
3. The game continues until everyone has had a turn at acting out.
4. The game can be followed by a circle time discussion on the issue of lying and the importance of telling the truth.

Variations

- A more straightforward version of the game is to have a child perform an action in the centre of the circle, then other children take turns to guess what action was being performed. The child who guesses correctly then takes a turn in the centre of the circle.
- If the children find it difficult to think of ideas to act out, then a selection of action cards could be made. The cards can be put into a bag or hat and pupils can choose a card before acting it out.

Name Game

Name Game is a simple circle time game which is a great ice-breaker. It is ideal for use at the beginning of a new school year as it helps children to learn the names of their classmates.

Suitable for

KS1, KS2

Aims

* To introduce and reinforce the rules and procedures of circle time.
* To help children to learn the names of all of their classmates.
* To identify and respect the differences and similarities between people.

Resources

* Circle time ball/object to signify whose turn it is

What to do

1. Have the children sit in a circle. Introduce and discuss the class circle time rules (see PSHE introduction for suggestions).

2. Explain to the children: 'When you receive the ball, say your name loudly and clearly, and then pass the ball on to the next person in the circle.'

3. Once all children have had their turn, explain: 'This time you need to say your name and tell everyone something that you like. This could be a hobby, interest, favourite lesson or even favourite food.'

4. Once all children have had their turn, a discussion can take place about how everyone in the class is unique, how it is good to find out things about each other and important to value the differences between us.

Variations

- The children can play Name Game, but have to say the name of the person sitting immediately on their left, rather than saying their own name when they get the ball. This can be followed by the children saying the name of the person on their right, and then the children can be asked to change places in the circle and play the game again from the beginning.
- Why not ask the pupils to say their name and try to express a given emotion when they say it, such as happiness, anger or sadness?

Parachute Ball Games

Parachute Ball Games are great fun to play for children of all ages. The children need to cooperate and work as a team to be successful. It is very important to remind children of your safety rules before taking the parachute out, e.g. remove shoes and socks if moving on top of the parachute, do not make physical contact with anybody if moving under the parachute, remove any jewellery, etc.

Suitable for

KS1, KS2

Aims

- To encourage the attitudes of teamwork and cooperation.
- To develop gross motor skills.
- To build muscles and improve coordination.

Resources

- Parachute and large, clear space indoors or outdoors
- Selection of balls/bean bags (depending on which games are played)

What to do

1. Invite the children to stand in a circle. You should remind the class of the parachute safety rules before unrolling the parachute.

2. The following games can be played in any order:

   A. *Flip*. All children hold the edge of the parachute. Roll a ball into the centre. The aim is to make the ball rise up into the air and flip off the parachute. The children will need to experiment as a team with different techniques to make these things happen.

You could add more balls, or different sized balls. If multiple balls are added, a time limit can be set to try and flip all of the balls off the parachute.

B. *Flip Catch*. Half of the children hold the edge of the parachute while the others stand around it. Roll a ball into the middle of the parachute. The aim is to flip the ball out of the parachute to be caught by one the children standing around the edge. When a child catches the ball, they can join the children in holding the edge of the parachute.

C. *Rollercoaster*. All children hold the edge of the parachute. Place the ball in front of one child. The aim is to make the ball travel all the way around the edge of the parachute. This game can be played sitting or standing, and the children may require several attempts before discovering how to accomplish the aim.

D. *Ball Keeper*. Some children stand or crouch under the parachute while the others hold the edge up at chest height. Roll several balls on to the parachute. The aim for children underneath is to knock the balls off it. The aim for those holding the edge is to keep the balls on the parachute.

Parachute Movement Games

Parachute Movement Games are great fun to play for children of all ages. The children need to cooperate and work as a team to be successful. It is very important to remind children of your safety rules before taking the parachute out, e.g. remove shoes and socks if moving on top of the parachute, do not make physical contact with anybody if moving under the parachute, remove any jewellery, etc.

Suitable for

KS1, KS2

Aims

- To encourage the attitudes of teamwork and cooperation.
- To develop gross motor skills.
- To improve coordination.

Resources

- Parachute and large, clear space indoors or outdoors

How to play

1. Invite the children to stand in a circle. Remind the class of the parachute rules before unrolling the parachute.

2. The following games can be played in any order:

   A. *Birthdays*. The children practise lifting the parachute up into the air as a team, holding the edge above their head. Call out the name of a month when the parachute is on the way up; any child with a birthday in that month goes under the parachute and moves into an empty space around the edge before the parachute falls. This type of game can be played by giving each child a number, colour or team, rather than using months as the signal to move. You can ask just the boys or the girls to change places, or the instruction 'All change' can be given. Always remind children to be careful to avoid collisions.

B. *Mexican Wave*. The children crouch while holding the edge of the parachute. Choose one child to stand quickly to begin a Mexican wave. The children jump up one by one in a clockwise direction to create the effect.

C. *Wave Maker*. All children sit holding the edge of the parachute. Tell the children that they are going to create the story of a storm. Ask the children to make gentle ripples on the surface by making small movements. This can then build up into huge crashing waves with large movements. A story about a storm could be read/made up, during which the children need to perform the correct movements at the appropriate time.

D. *Circus Tent*. The children hold the edge of the parachute, stand and lift it above their heads. The aim is for them to bring the parachute behind their heads and down until they can sit on the piece they were holding. This creates a 'circus tent'; one child can be chosen to go to the centre of the parachute to support it with their head to act as a tent pole! This provides an unusual and atmospheric feel for discussions or story-telling.

E. *Shark*. The children sit with their legs outstretched under the parachute while holding the edge. They make small waves by gently moving the edge up and down. One child is chosen to go under the parachute to become the shark; they move around and then tap one child on the leg. This child then goes under the parachute to become the shark, and the old shark takes their place around the edge. You can allow more than one shark to be under the parachute so long as the children are very careful not to make physical contact with each other.

Partner Time

> Partner Time is a series of listening games which can be played in their own right, or used as a variation for many other circle time games. The children will need to listen closely and cooperate with each other in order to complete the tasks.

Suitable for

KS1, KS2

Aims

- To develop one-on-one listening skills.
- To encourage children to learn and retain information about each other.
- To develop the attitude of teamwork.

Resources

- Circle time ball/object to signify whose turn it is
- Individual whiteboards and pens
- Secret shape/pattern/object/cards

What to do

1. Have the children sit in a circle and explain: 'Listening to and working together with a partner are both very important skills. We are going to play some games to help us develop these skills.'

2. The following games can be played in any order:

   A. *Favourites*. Put the children into pairs and ask them to learn what their partner's favourite colour is. The ball is then passed around the circle as each child says aloud what their partner's answer was. This game can be repeated for topics such as favourite TV programme, lesson, animal, etc.

B. *About My Partner.* Children are put into pairs and labelled as A or B. Child A is given one minute to learn as much information as possible about child B, i.e. favourite food, hobbies, music, or number of brothers and sisters, etc. Tell the children to change over once one minute has elapsed. Child B then learns about child A. The children then pass the ball around the circle, taking turns to share the information which they learned about their partner with the whole class.

C. *Secret Shapes.* Put the children into pairs and ask one of the children to turn and face away from the other. One child keeps a secret shape card hidden while the other holds the whiteboard and pen. The child with the secret shape card has to explain the secret shape in simple steps, while the other draws it on the whiteboard. After two minutes the children turn to face each other and compare the secret shape card and the whiteboard drawing. The pairs can then fetch a new secret shape card and change roles.

Variations

- If children are having difficulty remembering details about their partners when playing Partner Time games, then whiteboards could be used for them to note down their partners' answers.
- The results from games such as Favourites can be recorded in a tally chart and used in Numeracy lessons on data handling.

Secret Shapes Examples

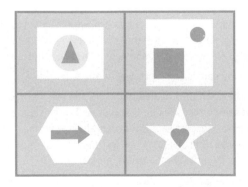

Roller Ball

Roller Ball is a simple circle time game in which children need to work together to help the ball travel around the circle. This game will develop gross motor skills (*which control big movements, using your body, arms and legs*).

Suitable for

KS1, KS2

Aims

- To develop gross motor skills.
- To build muscles and improve coordination.
- To develop the attitude of teamwork.

Resources

- Large ball/s (sponge ball/s for younger children)

What to do

1. Ask the children to sit in a circle.
2. Explain to the children: 'You need to sit with your legs outstretched and you might want to put your hands out behind you for stability. The ball needs to travel all the way around the circle without touching the floor. You are only allowed to use your legs to move it. You need to work as a team to stop the ball from touching the floor.'
3. Before starting the game, you may wish to lead a few leg-stretching exercises such as pointing toes away and then towards you or raising both legs off the ground together and slowly lowering them.
4. Once the game starts, you can choose whether to restart the game when the ball touches the floor, or to carry on from the point where it fell.

Variations

- A second ball can be added to the circle which can either move in the same or opposite direction as the first. The children can decide how to deal with a crossover!
- A time limit can be set for the ball to travel around the circle with a stopwatch or sand timer. The children can work towards this limit and then it could be lowered.
- Why not use a sound cue such as a whistle to signify that the ball needs to change direction?

Sentence Maker/Story Maker

Sentence Maker/Story Maker are fun Literacy-based games for use in circle time. Children take turns to build a sentence or story; this requires careful listening and quick thinking.

Suitable for

KS1, KS2

Aims

- To encourage listening skills.
- To develop understanding of sentence and story structure.
- To build personal confidence when speaking in circle time.

Resources

- Circle time ball/object to signify whose turn it is

What to do

1. Ask the children to sit in a circle and remind them of the circle time rules (see PSHE introduction for suggestions).

2. *Sentence Maker*. Explain to the children: 'I am going to start a sentence and then pass the ball to the person on my left. They will then say a word to continue the sentence and pass the ball on to the next person. You need to listen carefully to the sentence as it builds up and try to think of a word which makes sense when it is your turn. Remember that if you can't think of a word then you are welcome to pass and give the ball to the next person.'

3. Start the game with a phrase such as 'I was . . .', 'Their names were . . .' 'To my surprise . . .' or 'Once upon a time . . .'.

4. You may find that a new sentence needs to be started once one has come to an obvious end. With practice the children will begin to do this for themselves.

5. *Story Maker*. This follows the same procedure, but rather than adding one word, this time the children need to add a sentence each time it is their turn, attempting to keep the plot and characters consistent. The children could aim to bring the story to an end by the time it reaches the end of the circle.

Variations

- Children can repeat a given sentence or retell a familiar story to build confidence with the games until they are ready to create their own sentences and stories.
- A picture or pictorial storyboard could be displayed to give a structure to the sentences or stories.
- A completed sentence or the beginning of a story from the game could be recorded on a whiteboard and used as the starting point for a piece of writing/Literacy work.

Spiderweb

Spiderweb is a versatile and entertaining game where the children create a web using a ball of wool or string. It can be played in its own right or used as a variation for other circle time games.

Suitable for

KS1, KS2

Aims

- To ensure every child's involvement in circle time.
- To encourage concentration in circle time.
- To develop the attitude of teamwork.

Resources

- Ball/s of wool or string

What to do

1. Ask the children to form a circle and explain: 'I am going to give the ball of string to one person; they need to hold on to the end without letting go. They will then roll the ball of string to another person in the circle. This person will hold the string without letting go and roll/throw the ball of string on to another person'.

2. The spiderweb is built as the ball is passed to every member of the circle.

3. The last child to receive the ball can be given the job of retracing the string to carefully unravel the web.

Variations

- A second ball of string with a different colour can be added to the circle. Children are only allowed to hold one point of the spiderweb.
- Spiderweb can be played in conjunction with other circle time games such as I Think You're Great! or Emotions. Alternatively, the children could be asked to say their favourite food, colour or hobby when the ball of string reaches them.

The Memory Game

The Memory Game is a fun activity for use in circle time. Children will need to watch and listen with care if they are going to remember the choices of their classmates.

Suitable for

KS1, KS2

Aims

- To develop short-term memory.
- To improve speaking and listening skills.

Resources

- Circle time ball/object to signify whose turn it is
- Class set of whiteboards and pens (optional)

How to play

1. Invite the children to sit in a circle and remind the class of the circle time rules (see PSHE introduction for suggestions).

2. Explain to the children: 'I am going to say something which I like, e.g. "I like ice-cream," then I will pass the ball to the person on my left. They will say "ice-cream," and then they will add something which they like to the list, e.g. "ice-cream, I like football". The ball then gets passed on to the next person in the circle who will say "ice-cream, football," and then they will add their own choice.'

3. Before starting the game, you may wish to talk to the children about ways to help them remember the list such as looking at the other children when they say their choice, repeating the list in their head as other children recite it or associating the choice with the child by creating a mental picture.

> **4.** Once the game begins, you can choose whether to restart when a mistake is made, or to begin a new chain from that point.

Variations

- Once the children are confident with this game, they can then be called out if they make a mistake with the list, and the next person in the circle can take over.
- You should start each game from a different point in the circle to ensure that the children practise reciting lists of different lengths.
- The children can draw a picture and write the word of their choice on a small whiteboard to be held up in front of them until everyone has had their turn. The whiteboard can then be hidden and they have to try and recite the list. This variation can be a useful opportunity to discuss the different learning styles, i.e. visual, auditory and kinaesthetic.
- To simplify the game, why not split the class into smaller groups which move into their own space and play the game?

Guess My Job

Guess My Job is an interesting and motivating activity which encourages children to think about their future and the skills which they will need to pursue their chosen career.

Suitable for

KS1, KS2

Aims

- To help children understand the range of jobs carried out by people and how to develop their skills to make their own contribution in the future.
- To encourage children to recognise their strengths.
- To use dramatic techniques to convey actions and ideas.

Resources

- Circle time ball/object to signify whose turn it is
- A4 paper and pencils/whiteboards and pens (optional)

What to do

1. Have the children sit in a circle. Remind the class of the circle time rules (see PSHE introduction for suggestions).

2. Explain to the children: 'When you are older, you are going to choose the type of job that you want to do. What jobs do you know? Are there different types of job? Different jobs require different sets of skills, knowledge and qualities. When it is your turn, you need to go to the centre of the circle and act out the job which you would like to do when you are older. The other children will try and guess what it is that you are acting out. Once your chosen job is guessed or explained, then we will think about the skills, knowledge and qualities which you might need to do this job.' (The children could write these down on paper or whiteboards.)

3. Once several children have had their turn, it may be appropriate to discuss the fact that many jobs require lots of different skills, knowledge and qualities. For example: boys/girls wanting to become footballers will need to be good at more than just PE; they will need to have a good understanding of elements of science and maths, etc.

Variations

- The children could write up their jobs and the skills, knowledge and qualities required. This could be done by hand or using a computer, including pictures. The finished work can then be displayed to act as a motivational tool.
- Why not invite a selection of adults into school to talk about their careers with the children? The class could prepare appropriate interview questions beforehand.

The Feel-Good Factor

The Feel-Good Factor is an engaging activity which improves the self-esteem of every person involved. The children are always surprised to discover the good qualities others see in them.

Suitable for

KS2

Aims

- To encourage children to feel positive about themselves.
- To encourage children to find positive qualities in other people.
- To recognise the similarities and differences between people.

Resources

- A4 paper and pencils

What to do

1. Ask the children to sit in a circle, or two to three smaller circles and explain: 'We all know that everyone is unique, we all have different good and bad qualities. Today we are going to concentrate on our good qualities. Everyone needs to write their name at the top of their piece of paper. Your page will then be passed on to the person on your left; that person will write down something positive about you; it could be something they like about you, one of your positive qualities or something good you have done. It is important that you write your comments at the bottom of the page, fold the bottom of the page up to cover what you have written, and then pass the page on to the next person in the circle.'

2. The children stop when they have received their own Feel-Good Factor page. They can then go to their seat in the classroom and

unravel the page one comment at a time and discover what the other children have written about them.

3. A circle time discussion can follow, in which pupils can express how the activity made them feel and anything which surprised them.

Variations

- Some children may need assistance in the actual writing of their feel-good comments; others may need to see a selection of positive comments on the board to choose from initially.
- An alternative method is to use Post-it notes and allow the children to stick them on to each other once they have written positive comments on them.
- The Feel-Good Factor could be done on a daily/weekly basis where the whole class concentrates on one person at a time. This can be an extremely effective activity for children who need to build their self-esteem, or those who need to have their positive behaviour reinforced.

Chapter 8
Science

Science

In this section you will find lesson activities and ideas which develop children's scientific enquiry skills and their knowledge of life/physical processes, and materials and their properties.

The activities in this section have been selected because they provide good assessment and development opportunities for scientific enquiry skills (Sc1).

Science tips

- Invite children to perform actions wherever possible to represent scientific principles or processes.
- Use a digital camera to record stages in investigations and ask the children to provide a narration for the photo sequence.
- Try to set investigations in a real-life context.
- Ensure that the children possess the necessary investigative skills before asking them to complete an independent enquiry in full.

Animal Inventor

Animal Inventor is a fun activity which allows children to create a new animal. The children will need to use their knowledge of habitats and life processes to invent a plausible creature.

Suitable for

KS1, KS2

Aims

- To understand that animals are suited to their habitats/environments.
- To understand that the life processes of animals include nutrition, growth, movement and reproduction.
- To understand that senses enable animals to be aware of the world around them.

Resources

- Pictures/photographs/video of animals
- Drawing paper
- Pencils and coloured pencils

What to do

1. Introduce the activity by showing the children pictures, photographs or videos of animals with which the children are familiar. Ask the children a selection of ability-appropriate questions about the animals' habitat, diet, movement, senses and appearance.

2. Explain to the children: 'You are going to invent a new animal. You will need to think about habitat, senses, diet and appearance. Your animal must be suited to its environment. Once you have a good idea for your animal, you need to draw a picture of it in its habitat.

> You should label the picture with the animal's name and details about diet, senses, movement and appearance.'
>
> **3.** The children complete their animal invention drawings and share their work with the rest of the class.

Variations

- Why not ask more able children to create a food chain diagram which includes their invented animal?
- The children could create a model of their creature using clay or other modelling materials.
- You can set requirements for the children's animal inventions such as a specific habitat in which the creature must live or a specific species of animal.
- The children could be set the challenge of inventing two new animals: one predator and one prey.

Healthy Menu

Healthy Menu is an engaging activity in which children devise a menu which includes food from the major food groups and healthy options.

Suitable for

KS1, KS2

Aims

- To learn about the importance of an adequate and varied diet for health.
- To use observations and data to draw conclusions.

Resources

- Pictures/photographs of food
- Food eaten recording sheets (to be completed as homework)
- Menu grids

What to do

1. Introduce the topic by asking the children to record everything they eat and drink over one day. This can be done as homework, with the help of parents if necessary.

2. Use the data collected to introduce or consolidate learning on the food groups by asking the children to list everything they ate under one of these headings: Bread, Cereals and Potatoes/Fruit and Vegetables/Meat, Fish, Eggs and Alternatives/Milk and Dairy/Fats and Sugars. Ask the children to look at their results and draw any conclusions.

3. Lead a discussion on the importance of eating a healthy, varied and balanced diet.

4. Invite the children to work with a partner and create a healthy and balanced menu for either: a meal, a day or a week, depending on their ability. This menu could be created using pictures/drawings of the food or written on to a menu grid.

5. Invite the children to share their menu ideas and explain what makes theirs healthy, varied and balanced.

Variations

- Why not try to use the children's menus to plan the content of a school dinner or packed lunch in collaboration with the school kitchen or parents?
- The children could make and eat a healthy meal such as a nutritious sandwich in the classroom.
- The children could make healthy eating posters to display around the school.
- Why not incorporate a visit to a local supermarket to discuss how to identify healthy food?

Name: Bethany

Menu Grid

Meal Grid	Breakfast	Lunch	Dinner	Snacks
Description	Bran Flakes, Clementine Juice, Milk	Baked Potato	Some chicken soup, Bread	Banana Bread, Banana, Chocolate, Some Buiscuits
Food Groups	Protien, Milk, chicken, Soup.	Fat and Sugar, chocolate, Buiscuits	Carbohydrate, Bread, Toast, Bran-flakes, Banana-Bread, Potato.	Vegtable + fruit. Clementine, Juice, Banana, Apple. Salad

These and additional images are available to view/download from the companion website at **www.pearsoned.co.uk/barron**.

Sense It

Sense It is a practical and memorable activity which children will enjoy. They will need to use their senses to discover the identity of a variety of concealed items.

Suitable for

KS1, KS2

Aims

- To understand that senses enable humans and other animals to be aware of the world around them.
- To use scientific language to describe things and communicate ideas.
- To draw conclusions from observations and other data.

Resources

- Mystery box (sealable box with an opening on the side big enough for a child's hand)
- Selection of objects to go inside the mystery box
- Blindfolds
- Selection of food and drink to be tasted
- Selection of items for smelling
- Recording grid/paper and pencils
- Selection of items which make a noise or recording of noises

What to do

1. Introduce the activity by asking the children to share their knowledge about the five senses which we use. The class could discuss the effects of sensory deprivation on people and the terms which relate to this, e.g. deaf/blind.

2. Explain to the children: 'We are going to discover how good our senses are by playing a game called Sense It. This game is made

up of several activities, some of which you will carry out with a partner. The activities will require concentration and cooperation as sometimes you or your partner will be blindfolded.'

3. Introduce the following activities in any order:

   A. *Touch.* Conceal an object in the mystery box. The children take turns to put their hands inside the box and work out what the object is, using touch alone. You can change the object each time, or tell the children to keep their answer a secret until everyone has had their turn. If there is a large group of children, it may be advisable to use two or more mystery boxes.

   B. *Taste.* The children work in pairs. Child A wears a blindfold while child B carefully feeds child A with a small amount of appropriate foodstuffs. You need to be fully aware of any allergies which the children have. Child A describes and tastes the food, and then gives an answer/name of the food which they think they have tasted. The blindfold is removed and the foodstuff is revealed to Child A. The children swap roles and use a different foodstuff. Each child could have their own plastic spoon which they use when tasting the food.

   C. *Smell.* The children work in pairs. Child A wears a blindfold while child B carefully holds an item under the nose of child A. Child A gently smells the item and gives a description and answer/name of the item. The blindfold is removed and the item is revealed to Child A. The children swap roles and use a different item.

   D. *Hearing.* Create different sounds with their sources hidden. This can be done by making the sounds behind a screen or recording them prior to the lesson and playing them back to the children. The children record their ideas for the sound sources in a list. You can also ask the children to describe the sounds they hear. The sound sources are revealed to the children; they could share their ideas/answers before each sound is revealed.

   E. *Sight.* Ask the children to cover their ears with their hands. Say a sentence or phrase while using appropriate body language and facial expression. This phrase can be repeated several times. The children write down what they think you were saying. Repeat the phrase after the children have shared some of their ideas on what was being said.

4. Following on from these activities, a discussion can take place about the importance and significance of our senses, how we react when some of our senses are deprived and how our senses work together.

Variations

- You can make many of the Sense It activities easier by offering the children multiple choice answers for the sense tests before they are carried out.

Conductor or Insulator

Conductor or Insulator invites children to predict and then test whether a range of materials will conduct electricity or act as an insulator.

Suitable for

KS2

Aims

- To understand that some materials are better electrical conductors than others.
- To use observations and data to draw conclusions.

Resources

- Simple circuit components – batteries and holders, bulbs and holders, wires with crocodile clips, etc.
- A range of test materials
- Recording grids and pencils

What to do

1. Introduce the topic by discussing the terms 'conductor' and 'insulator'. Set up a simple circuit with a battery, bulb and wires with a break between two crocodile clips. Allow the children to observe the bulb lighting when the crocodile clips are connected to form a complete circuit. Disconnect the crocodile clips and explain that materials can be put into the space to test their conductivity.

2. Explain to the children: 'We are going to test a range of materials to find out if they are conductors or insulators. If the bulb lights, then the material is an electrical conductor; if the bulb does not

light, then it is an insulator. How are you going to make it a fair test? What do you predict will happen? How will you record your results?'

3. Ensure that the children test their circuit to make sure that it lights the bulb before beginning their investigation.

4. Allow the children to predict outcomes, test the materials and record their results in a suitable table. Ask the children to draw conclusions with a partner before discussing the findings as a group.

5. Discuss the practical implications of the investigation findings, i.e. why certain materials are used for specific purposes (electrical cable, plug, etc.) because of their properties.

Variations

- The children could test materials which they find in the classroom as well as the materials provided by you.
- The children could draw a circuit diagram using the correct symbols.
- More able children can predict and test what happens when components such as extra bulbs or batteries are added to the circuit.

Plants

Here you will find a selection of practical activities which focus on plants and their functions. The children will enjoy planting, examining, observing and making conclusions based on their investigations.

Suitable for

KS2

Aims

- To understand that seeds grow into flowering plants.
- To find out about the different kinds of plants and animals in the local environment.
- To recognise that the life processes common to plants include growth, nutrition and reproduction.
- To recognise and name the leaves, flowers, stems and roots of flowering plants.
- To understand that it is important to test ideas using evidence from observation and measurement.
- To use observations and data to draw conclusions.

Resources

Depending on the activity chosen you may need:

- Plant pots or suitable containers
- Soil/potting compost
- Black sugar paper
- Various seeds
- Tomato plants
- Labels
- Clipboards
- Watering can

What to do

Choose from the following list of activities those which are suitable for your learning objective and appropriate for the ability level of your children. Always remind children to wash their hands after handling plants, leaves or soil.

A. *Plant Survey.* Allow the children to explore the school grounds or local area (with appropriate supervision). They should make sketches and notes about the different types of plants and trees they find. Pupils can then share their findings with the class and begin to identify the diversity of plant species and the similarities and differences between them.

B. *Growing from Seed.* Children love to see plants grow from seeds in the classroom. Use plastic cups or any suitable pot for growing the seeds and remember to get the children to label the pots with their names. Sunflower seeds are ideal for this purpose. Encourage the children to look after their plant by watering and choosing a good location for it in the classroom. You might like to measure the plants on a daily or weekly basis and record the data.

C. *Water.* Children will quickly learn that plants need water to survive if they set up a group experiment with two young tomato plants, one which will be watered and the other not. Decide with the children how you are going to make the test fair, i.e. using the same sized plants and pots, putting the plants in the same location, using the same amount of soil, etc. Encourage the class to make predictions on what they think will happen. It may take up to a week before the plant with no water begins to show a noticeable difference. Remember to clearly label the plant which is to have no water, and emphasise that the other plant must not be over-watered.

D. *Light.* Compare the effects of light on plants by using young tomato plants in the same way as activity C (Water). This time both plants should receive equal watering, but one should be completely covered to block out light. An easy way of doing this is to make cone shapes using two layers of black sugar paper or card.

E. *Temperature.* Examine the effects of temperature on plants by using tomato plants in the same way as activities C and D. This time one of the plants should be kept in a fridge while the other stays at room temperature.

F. *Nutrients.* This investigation will demonstrate that plants need nutrients (minerals) to grow well. The children should plant broad bean seeds in a variety of growing materials such as sand, grit, different soils (you could ask the children to bring in soil from their garden), sawdust, cotton wool, etc. Decide with the children how the test will be kept fair, i.e. same location, same amount of water, same sized pots, etc. Discuss how the children are going to judge the healthiness of the plants and how they are going to record their data before and during the investigation. Once the plants show obvious differences, you should discuss the reasons why and compare the results with the children's predictions.

G. *Plant Parts.* Collect a variety of plants and flowers for the children to examine. Invite them to draw and label any parts of the plants which they know the names and functions of. Collect the children's ideas and go on to correct any misconceptions. Explain the functions of leaves, roots, stems and flowers at an appropriate level for your children's ability. Repeat the drawing and labelling activity as an assessment opportunity.

H. *Plants for Food.* To show the process of plants being grown for food, why not grow herbs or vegetables from seed at school? This is a long-term project which requires careful planning and maintenance, but the learning and sense of satisfaction which the children will get from eating their own produce will more than justify the effort. There are many plants suitable for this project including carrots, peas, spinach, coriander, tomatoes, etc. Why not let the children choose what it is they would like to grow, and cultivate a selection by sowing seeds, transplanting them and harvesting? If there is a lack of suitable space at school, then try approaching the nearest allotment. There are numerous organisations which offer advice and support. The children could plan to incorporate their produce into a meal which could be prepared for a school dinner.

Pulse Rate

Pulse Rate is an activity where children learn about how the pulse rate changes when exercising and resting. The children complete a number of exercises and interpret their findings.

Suitable for

KS2

Aims

* To understand the effect of exercise and rest on pulse rate.
* To use observations and data to draw conclusions.

Resources

* Stopwatches
* Recording grids and pencils
* Large clear space for exercising
* Skipping ropes

What to do

1. Introduce the topic by discussing the functions of the heart, i.e. the heart pumps blood around the body through arteries and veins; each time the heart pumps we can feel this in the neck or wrist and this is called a pulse or heartbeat.

2. Demonstrate how to find a pulse using several fingers on the wrist or neck and ask the children to carefully locate their pulse. Try asking them to measure their pulse for 30 seconds by counting the number of beats, and then double the results to find the number of beats per minute. The average resting heart rate is between 70 and 80 beats per minute.

3. Explain to the children: 'We are going to find out what happens to our pulse rate when we exercise our bodies. We will measure our resting heart rate before we begin and then measure it again when we have completed each exercise for one minute. The exercises we will do are walking, jogging, star jumps and skipping. Can you predict what will happen to your pulse rate?'

4. The children can work in pairs with a stopwatch to measure their pulse rates and record their data in a suitable table.

5. Discuss the data collected and the reasons why the pulse rate increased during exercise. Ask the children to use their data to write up their conclusions.

Variations

- The children could use the data to create a line graph to show their results.
- Why not continue to investigate how long it takes for the heart rate to return to its resting rate after exercising?

Example Recording Grid

Name:	BPM ♥
Rest	
Walking	
Jogging	
Star jumps	
Skipping	

These and additional images are available to view/download from the companion website at **www.pearsoned.co.uk/barron**.

Chapter 9
Display

Display

This section contains some good ideas for essential and useful classroom wall displays. The learning environment is a crucial part of an effective classroom. High-quality displays can assist with classroom organisation, show that the children's work is valued and act as teaching aids, as well as making the classroom an exciting and inviting place in which to learn.

General display tips

- **Use all available spaces for display.** Hang things from the ceiling, attach washing lines, use the windows.
- **Keep a set of good-quality tools together in a box away from the children.** Staple gun, hand stapler, staples, staple remover, pliers, string, scissors, Blu-Tack, glue, pins, etc.
- **Use fabrics and unusual materials.** Using a range of materials will lift a display and add interest. Try cardboard, bubble wrap or gift wrap for backing or mounting.
- **Use questions to engage children.** Why not relate display questions to your topic objectives? Alternatively, try displaying questions the children have about the subject and add the answers as the topic progresses.
- **Add key words.** Display key vocabulary with definitions and pictures as it becomes useful in the topic.
- **Give the class different sizes, shapes and colours of paper to work on for the same project.** This appeals to the children and adds interest to a display of the work.
- **Use layers.** Add depth to your displays by attaching large shapes to the display backing in a different colour. Try using two or three different colour strips to create the backing.
- **Be creative.** Think of exciting titles for your displays; sometimes a question works well. Don't be afraid to place objects at strange angles or tear the edges of backing materials rather than cutting.
- **Get help.** From children, parents or teaching assistants. Try asking the pupils what colours they would like to use on the classroom displays.

All About Us

> A display which shows photos and details of all members of the class.

Suitable for

KS1, KS2

Aims

* To encourage the children to think about themselves and why they are unique.
* To help children and staff learn the names of those in the class
* To reinforce and display whole class or personal targets.

Suggestions|Ideas|Contents

1. Photograph of each child. The children can be asked to bring into school something important to them to be photographed with, i.e. a favourite book, toy, instrument or sports item.
2. The children can handwrite or word process a name label with special or unique details about themselves and the item which they have been photographed with.
3. Once displayed, the photographs and details about each child make a useful site for adding personal or whole class targets which can be changed or marked when they are achieved.
4. The All About Us display could also be a used as a part of the class reward/behaviour system, by adding stickers or stars around the photos for special achievements.
5. It is a good idea to have a photograph of the class teacher and any teaching assistants who work in the class on this display.
6. The creation of this display is a useful activity for the first days of a new school year. When the display is taken down, the photographs and accompanying writing could be added to the children's records of achievement, or sent on to the next class teacher.

Art Gallery

A display which shows pieces of art, including work completed at home or at school, and the work of other artists.

Suitable for

KS1, KS2

Aims

- To value and display children's artwork.
- To allow all children to have work displayed in the classroom.

Suggestions/Ideas/Contents

1. Display artwork the children have completed at home or at school.
2. Display copies of artwork/pictures/adverts which the children bring in from home. Discuss these with the class, including the reasons why they like them.
3. Display photographs taken by the children outside school.
4. Display photographs of 3D artwork made at school.
5. Why not ask the children to vote for their favourite piece of artwork and award a prize?

Class Notice-board

A Class Notice-board is an essential display for teachers, parents, children and visitors to the classroom.

Suitable for

KS1, KS2

Aims

- To inform children of the weekly timetable.
- To remind children and parents about important events.
- To remind children to remember essential items.

Suggestions/Ideas/Contents

1. Weekly class lesson timetable, ideally with accompanying pictures/symbols to represent each lesson.
2. PE kit reminder – 'Remember to bring your PE kit on Tuesday'; accompany with a picture.
3. Musical instrument reminder – 'Remember to bring your recorder on Friday'; accompany with a picture.
4. Copies of weekly planning for reference by supply teachers or teaching assistants.
5. Spare copies of homework and school letters.
6. Photographs of recent activities.

Thought of the Week

A Thought of the Week display is a useful tool for encouraging positive actions, good behaviour and thoughtful responses. It can be used in conjunction with PSHE or circle time.

Suitable for

KS1, KS2

Aims

- To encourage personal thoughts, interpretation, reflection and responses to a statement.
- To recognise how behaviour affects other people.
- To listen to other people, and play and work cooperatively.
- To identify and respect the differences and similarities between people.

Suggestions/Ideas/Contents

1. Thought of the Week is a simple display on which a statement from the list below should be shown in large lettering. The statement or thought should be discussed with the children and referred to throughout the week. It could be introduced at the beginning of the week and reviewed at the end.
2. This display could be situated in a position where it can be easily viewed during circle time sessions. Alternatively, a good position for this display is near or on the back of the classroom door: this means that the children will see it whenever they leave the classroom.
3. An idea for creating this display is: a large picture of a head with a thought bubble extending to a whiteboard or a space where a printed thought can be attached.
4. Suggestions for Thought of the Week:
   - Patience is a virtue.
   - If at first you don't succeed – try, try, try again.
   - Laughter is the best medicine.

- When you believe, you can achieve.
- Good manners cost nothing.
- If you don't have a smile, I'll give you one of mine.
- The only way to have a friend is to be one.
- How I look is not as important as how I act.
- I treat others the way I would like them to treat me.
- Each day offers a new chance to do your best.
- Think before you act.
- A good sport follows the rules, takes turns and plays fair.
- Treat everyone with respect.
- Honesty is the best policy.
- You only get one body, so take care of it.
- Even though I make mistakes, I can do lots of things well.
- Don't limit your challenges, challenge your limits.
- All things are difficult before they are easy.
- No act of kindness, no matter how small, is ever wasted.

5. The Thought of the Week display can be changed to Thought of the Day, Month or Term.

Where in the World?

A useful map-based display to broaden children's understanding of the world.

Suitable for

KS1, KS2

Aims

- To familiarise children with the countries and continents of the world.
- To develop children's knowledge and awareness of other countries.
- To help children to understand the location of areas present in current news stories.

Suggestions/Ideas/Contents

1. A large world map should be mounted at the centre of the display board. This leaves space around the edge for attaching postcards brought in by children or staff to indicate places they have visited.
2. Notes can also be added around the map to show the location of areas which are in the news, or are of importance to topics being studied at school.
3. It is a good idea to include facts about each new location next to the postcards, and discuss each postcard with the class as it is added to the display.
4. String can be trailed from the postcard to the appropriate spot on the map and secured with a drawing pin, or alternatively colour-coded stickers/dots can be used.
5. A useful addition to this display could be an enlarged map of the school's local area, or the United Kingdom.

Where in the world?

Chapter 10
Reward Games & Early Morning Work

Reward Games & Early Morning Work

In this section you will find versatile activities, games and ideas which can be used as rewards for good behaviour/work. They can be used as settling activities for children to complete when they arrive at school in the morning or simply as time fillers for those rare occasions when you have a few minutes to spare!

The children will enjoy the games in this section, and quite often they will not realise that they are learning valuable lessons by playing them.

Once the children are familiar with several of the activities, you might like to let them choose one for the class to do. Why not encourage the children to develop their own classroom games and try them out with the class?

Dictionary Game

Dictionary Game is an educational game which is fun to play and encourages children to think about the meaning of words. Children of all abilities can be involved in the same game.

Suitable for

KS1, KS2

Aims

- To develop an understanding of the meaning of words.
- To understand and use a dictionary.
- To identify initial sounds in words.

Resources

- Dictionary (appropriate for ability of children)
- Scoreboard/whiteboard

What to do

1. Divide the class into two teams. Boys against girls is a quick way of doing this if appropriate in your class.

2. Choose a child to keep the score and ask them to draw a tally chart with two columns on the board.

3. Explain to the children: 'The rules for Dictionary Game are: I will choose one boy and one girl to come to the front of the class to represent their team. I will ask another person to choose a letter from the alphabet and tell me a word which begins with that letter, e.g. "s" for snake. I will then turn to the letter "s" in the dictionary and choose a word. I will read out the definition of the word twice,

and the boy and girl at the front will have 20 seconds in which to tell me what the word is. Whoever guesses the word correctly wins one point for their team, and they get to stay on for the next round. I will choose someone to replace the other player and the next round will begin. The winning team is the one with the most points at the end of the game.'

Variations

- When a letter has been chosen for a round of the game, why not ask the children which half of the dictionary the letter is from, i.e. the first half a – m or the second half n – z?
- You could allow a child to choose the words from the dictionary and read out the definition.
- You may like to introduce some additional rules such as: the players at the front have only one guess each/if both players guess incorrectly then someone with their hand up will be given a chance/if both players answer correctly at the same time then both teams get a point and a different definition will be read for the same players/if anyone tries to shout out the answer then their team loses a point.
- The children could have whiteboards and, when the letter is chosen, they have to write down three words which begin with that letter.

Eyewitness

Eyewitness is an entertaining game where the children witness a series of events. The challenge is for them to remember as much detail about the events as they can.

Suitable for

KS1, KS2

Aims

* To develop short-term memory skills.

Resources

* Individual whiteboards or paper

What to do

1. Explain to the children: 'One person called "Mr X" or "Miss. X" is going to leave the classroom. When they return they are going to do several things while we watch. As an eyewitness you need to try to remember what they do in as much detail as possible.'

2. You may wish to be Mr/Miss X, leaving and returning to the classroom yourself for the first game to model the kind of actions which are suitable, i.e. opening a window, turning a tap on and off, talking to a child, reading a book, putting a pen in your pocket, etc.

3. Once Mr/Miss X has finished, they need to leave the classroom again to indicate this.

4. The eyewitnesses then have to write down what happened in as much detail as possible.

5. When the children have finished writing you can ask questions such as:

- 'What was the first thing that Mr/Miss X did?'
- 'What clothing was Mr/Miss X wearing?'
- 'What did Mr/Miss X put in their pocket?'
- 'Who did Mr/Miss X talk to?'
- 'What did Mr/Miss X say?'
- 'How long was Mr/Miss X in the classroom for?'

Variations

- Why not ask the eyewitnesses to write down their answers to the questions and compare these at the end?
- Try asking some leading questions to see if the children create false memories, e.g. 'What colour were Mr/Miss X's gloves?' (when Mr/Miss X was not wearing any).
- Try allowing Mr/Miss X to change their appearance before entering the classroom.

Funny Faces

 Funny Faces is a simple game where children attempt to make each other laugh in various ways.

Suitable for

KS1, KS2

Aims

* To encourage children to play together confidently.
* To develop speaking and listening skills.

Resources

* Children's joke book (optional)

What to do

1. Divide the class into pairs. Explain to the children: 'You are going to take turns to try and make each other laugh! You are allowed to make funny faces or tell jokes to your partner, but you are not allowed to touch them.'

2. While one child pulls funny faces and tells jokes, the other must try not to laugh or smile for as long as possible. Once they do, then the partners change roles.

3. After a few turns the children can find a new partner and play again.

Variations

- Why not allow some children to use a joke book if they find it difficult to remember jokes themselves?
- At the end of the session you could ask the children to retell the funniest jokes they heard.
- You may wish to include a rule that the child keeping a serious face is not allowed to close their eyes!

Good Afternoon...

Good Afternoon... is a fun game where a child has to guess who it was that spoke to them.

Suitable for

KS1, KS2

Aims

* To develop speaking and listening skills.
* To encourage children to learn the names of their classmates.

Resources

* None

What to do

1. Choose a child to stand at the front of the class, facing away from the other children.

2. Explain to the children: 'I am going to point at someone in the class. They have to say "Good Afternoon..." followed by the name of the person at the front with their back to us. The person at the front has one go at guessing who it was that spoke to them.'

3. Children who get it right have another go, but if they get it wrong they change places with the person who spoke to them.

4. If a child gets it right five times in a row, ask them to choose another person to come to the front.

Variations

* A funny alternative is to allow the children to try and disguise their voices to fool the person at the front.

- Why not change the 'Good-afternoon' phrase to a funny one?
- You could allow a child to point and choose the person who speaks.
- Try giving the person at the front more than one guess to make the game easier.

Heads Down, Thumbs Up

Heads down, Thumbs Up is a popular classroom game which children of all ages will enjoy. The playing team tag children who will take turns to guess who tagged them.

Suitable for

KS1, KS2

Aims

- To move quietly around the classroom.
- To improve listening skills.

Resources

- None

What to do

1. Choose the team of players: this can be two to four children, who come to the front of the class.

2. Explain to the children: 'Everyone sitting at their desks needs to put their head down on the table, close their eyes and hold their thumbs up at the side of their head. The team will creep around the classroom and touch one person each on their thumbs. Once they have all tagged somebody the team will come back to the front and I will say, "Heads up." If you have been tagged you will stand up and you will get one guess as to who it was that tagged you. The team will keep quiet until everyone has guessed and then they will reveal if the guesses were right.'

3. Children who get it right will take the place of the player on the team; otherwise the players have another go.

Variations

- The children who are on the team when the game ends could be on the team when you next play Heads Down, Thumbs Up.

Missing Person

> Missing Person is a great game where a child hides and another has to play detective and work out who is missing.

Suitable for

KS1, KS2

Aims

- To develop speaking and listening skills.
- To develop memory and observation skills.
- To encourage children to learn the names of their classmates.

Resources

- Stopwatch (optional)

What to do

1. Explain to the children: 'I am going to choose one person to leave the room. I will then choose another person who will hide somewhere in the classroom out of view. The other children will all change seats before we ask the detective to come back in. The detective gets 30 seconds to work out who is missing and one guess, before the person hiding comes out.'
2. Children who get it right have another go, but if they get it wrong they change places with the person who was hiding.
3. If a child gets it right three times in a row, ask them to choose another person to leave the room and be the detective.

Variations

- You could allow the detective to ask for a clue as to the identity of the missing person.

- Why not have two children hide in the classroom?
- You can increase or decrease the time limit to make the game easier or harder.

Now You See It, Now You Don't

Now You See It, Now You Don't is a fun memory game. The children have one minute to memorise a group of objects.

Suitable for

KS1, KS2

Aims

- To develop short-term memory skills.

Resources

- Selection of 10 to 20 random objects
- Tray
- Towel
- Small whiteboards/paper for children

What to do

1. Place a selection of 10 to 20 random objects on a tray and cover them up with a towel, e.g. key, pencil, orange, cup, etc.
2. Explain to the children: 'You will have one minute to try and remember as many of the items on the tray as you can. Once the minute is up, I will cover the items again and you will write down all those which you can remember on your whiteboard.'
3. Remove the towel and insist that the children are quiet to allow everyone to concentrate for the entire minute.

4. Once the children have written their lists (you might want to set a time limit for this), you can reveal the items and total the children's scores. The winner is the child who remembered the most correct items.

5. Discuss the children's lists: Are there any items which all of the children forgot, and why? Is there anything we could do next time to help us remember the items?

Variations

- Why not teach the children some memory techniques such as visualisation, chaining or acrostics before playing the game.
- You could award a prize for the child who gets the most correct items.
- Try asking a child to choose the objects and lead the game.
- A variation of this game is to show the items for one minute, then cover and remove one or more items from the tray. Reveal the items again, and the winner is the first child to work out what is missing.
- You can make the game easier or harder by using fewer or more items on the tray and by increasing or decreasing the viewing times.

The Daily Edit

 The Daily Edit is an educational game in which children need to spot and correct the mistakes in a piece of writing.

Suitable for

KS1, KS2

Aims

- To recognise and use spelling patterns.
- To use punctuation appropriately.
- To recognise and correct common mistakes or omissions in written work.

Resources

- Piece of text with mistakes and omissions displayed on the whiteboard
- Paper/writing books

What to do

1. Write on the board or display a piece of text which contains several mistakes and omissions.

2. Explain to the children: 'You need to rewrite the text from the board correcting any mistakes you spot and adding anything which has been missed out. The mistakes could be in the spelling of words or the wrong punctuation; the missing things could be punctuation or whole words.'

3. You might need to demonstrate by correcting mistakes and omissions in the first sentence until the children are familiar with the activity.

4. Give the children a time limit for The Daily Edit. Once this time is up, correct the mistakes on the board by asking for the children's suggestions to begin with.

Variations

- Try asking the children to total how many corrections they made correctly and award a prize for the children with the most.
- You could ask a child to write the piece of text with mistakes for The Daily Edit.
- The genre of the text can be varied to suit current types of text being studied, e.g. newspaper report/fairy-tale/diary, etc.
- The word/sentence level mistakes can be linked to current word/sentence level objectives, e.g. missing double consonants/missing silent letters, etc.

Word Finder

Word Finder is an enjoyable educational game where children try to find as many words as they can using a given string of letters.

Suitable for

KS1, KS2

Aims

- To recognise the spelling of words.
- To develop word-building skills.
- To use a dictionary to check spellings.

Resources

- Dictionaries (appropriate for ability of children)
- Whiteboard/flipchart
- Small whiteboards/paper for children

What to do

1. Write a random string of letters on the whiteboard including both vowels and consonants, e.g. *d s a p o b m w n l e i g*.

2. Remind the children, if necessary, how to use a dictionary to check the spelling of a word.

3. Explain to the children: 'You have five minutes to make as many words as you can using the letters on the board. Write your words on a whiteboard and check the spelling of each word using a dictionary. The winner will be the one with the most correctly spelt words once the time is up.'

4. You might want to allow partners to check and total the scores, or you could ask the children to read out their words and write a list of them on the whiteboard.

Variations

- Why not limit the words to only those which have four letters or more?
- You could award a prize for the child who gets the most correctly spelt words, or for the child who gets the longest word.
- Choose whether or not you will allow the letters to be used more than once in a word.
- Try asking the children to make a sentence including the words which they have identified.
- You could include letters in the list which match the current focus for word level work or spellings, e.g. *ing* endings/*pl* prefix.
- Try asking a child to suggest the letters for the letter string at the beginning of the game.

20 Questions

20 Questions is a great game for children to play. It encourages thinking skills and develops speaking and listening. 20 Questions can be used to consolidate learning from topics being taught in class.

Suitable for

KS1, KS2

Aims

- To ask questions to clarify understanding.
- To relate contributions to what has gone on before.
- To listen to others.

Resources

- Whiteboard/flipchart to record question tally
- Small whiteboard to record the object/person/answer etc.

What to do

1. Explain to the children: 'I am going to allow you to have 20 questions. You will take turns to ask a question with the goal of finding out *what* or *who* it is that I have written down on my whiteboard and turned over. You will need to listen carefully to each other's questions and the answers if you are going to guess correctly before the questions run out. If you guess the word before the questions run out then you win; if you don't guess correctly then I win.'

2. Write down a word, choose a child to keep the score in the form of a tally chart on the whiteboard and highlight when the children ask good/appropriate questions.

3. The choice of words can be linked to topics being studied (e.g. Henry VIII, Mars, Synagogue), or be completely random. You might begin by telling the children whether the word is a person, object, place, etc.

Variations

- Why not ask a child to think of the word and answer the questions? It may be advisable to have them share their choice with you before the game begins.
- You can specify when the children are able to guess the word, e.g. after ten questions have been asked/when they are completely sure at any point/when they hold up two hands to show that they want to guess the word rather than ask a question.

Index of activities

Name of activity	Larger space required	Quick starter potential	Longer project potential
Amazing Buildings			✓
Adverts			✓
Album Artwork			✓
All About Us			
Animal Inventor			✓
Archery			
Art Gallery			✓
Artefact Explorers			
Band Race	✓		
Beat It!			
Bingo		✓	
Body Sounds			
Broadcast			✓
Build a Wall			
Cat and Mouse	✓		
Catch You Out		✓	
Character Conversations			
Character Letters			
Character Pie			
Character Rating			
Class Notice-board			
Coat of Arms			✓
Code Breakers			
Colours	✓	✓	
Compass Jumps		✓	
Conductor or Insulator			
Counting Actions		✓	
Counting Stick Games		✓	
Creative Writing Themes			
CV Building			
Detective			
Dictionary Game			

Name of activity	Larger space required	Quick starter potential	Longer project potential
Emotions			
Environmental Projects			✓
Eyewitness			
Follow the Drum	✓		
Frame It			✓
Freeze-Frame			
Function Machine			
Funny Faces			
Good Afternoon...		✓	
Grid Painting	✓		
Grid Problem			
Guess My Job			
Guess My Number			
Guess My Rule			
Guess My Shape			
Guided Mime			
Guided Reading (15 Activities)			
Guided Reading Questions			
Heads Down, Thumbs Up		✓	
Heads or Tails			
Healthy Menu			
History Day			✓
Hot-Seat			✓
I Think You're Great!		✓	
Illuminated Names			
In Between Scenes			
Keep it Up	✓		
Language Challenge (MFL) (5 Activities)			
Liar, Liar!	✓		
Magic Carpet			✓
Making the Rules			
Metal vs. Wood			
Missing Numbers			

Name of activity	Larger space required	Quick starter potential	Longer project potential
Missing Person			
Missing Sequence			
Money Maker			✓
Mood Music			✓
Music Glossary			
Musical Moves			
Musical Words			✓
Name Game			
Name That Instrument			
Nature Collage			✓
Now You See It, Now You Don't			
Number Shapes			
Number Tennis			
Numbers	✓	✓	
Orienteering	✓		✓
Parachute Ball Games	✓		
Parachute Movement Games	✓		
Partner Time			
Pass The Beat			
Pirates	✓		
Plants (8 Activities)			✓
Points of View			
Pulse Points			
Pulse Rate			
Puppet Stories			✓
Quiet Time			
Real Life Paintings	✓		✓
Remote Control	✓		
Roller Ball	✓		
Self-Portrait (5 Activities)			✓
Sense It			
Sentence Maker/Story Maker			
Shake, Strike or Blow			

Name of activity	Larger space required	Quick starter potential	Longer project potential
Silent Tambourine		✓	
Skylines			
Snakes	✓		
Snapshot			
Sound Pictures			
Sound Walk			
Soundscape			
Soundtrack			✓
Special Books			✓
Spiderweb			
Standing Rule			
Story Music			✓
Story Sequencing (5 Activities)			
Strange Surroundings			
Syllable Patterns			
Take me There			
The Bean Game	✓		
The Daily Edit			
The Feel-Good Factor			
The Memory Game			
Thought of the Week			✓
Time Machine			✓
Traffic Lights	✓		
Treasure Hunter	✓		
Uniform			✓
Ways to Play			
What Happens Next?			
What's Happening?			
Where In the World?			✓
Word Finder			
20 Questions		✓	

Classroom Gems

Innovative resources, inspiring creativity across the school curriculum

Designed with busy teachers in mind, the Classroom Gems series draws together an extensive selection of practical, tried-and-tested, off-the-shelf ideas, games and activities, guaranteed to transform any lesson or classroom in an instant.

© 2008 Paperback 336pp
ISBN: 9781405873925

© 2009 Paperback 312pp
ISBN: 9781408223260

© 2009 Paperback 216pp
ISBN: 9781408220382

© 2009 Paperback 232pp
ISBN: 9781408225578

© 2009 Paperback 384pp
ISBN: 9781408224359

© 2009 Paperback 392pp
ISBN: 9781408223208

© 2009 Paperback 320pp
ISBN: 9781408228098

© 2009 Paperback 352pp
ISBN: 9781408223291

© 2009 Paperback 192pp
ISBN: 9781408225608

'Easily navigable, allowing teachers to choose the right activity quickly and easily, these invaluable resources are guaranteed to save time and are a must-have tool to plan, prepare and deliver first-rate lessons'

PEARSON